Y0-BUY-571

ADOPTING
FROM
LATIN AMERICA

An AGENCY Perspective

ADOPTING FROM LATIN AMERICA

An AGENCY Perspective

By

JAMES A. PAHZ, Ed.D., M.P.H.

Associate Professor of Public Health Education
Central Michigan University
Mt. Pleasant, Michigan

Executive Director
Children's Hope Adoption Service
Shepherd, Michigan

CHARLES C THOMAS · PUBLISHER
Springfield · Illinois · U.S.A.

Published and Distributed Throughout the World by

CHARLES C THOMAS • PUBLISHER

2600 South First Street

Springfield, Illinois 62794-9265

© *1988 by* CHARLES C THOMAS • PUBLISHER

ISBN 0-398-05492-4

Library of Congress Catalog Card Number: 88-4929

Printed in the United States of America

Q-R-3

Library of Congress Cataloging in Publication Data

Pahz, James Alon.
  Adopting from Latin America.

  Bibliography: p.
  Includes index.
  1. Intercountry adoption--United States. 2. Children
--Latin America. I. Title.
HV875.55.P34   1988   362.7'34'0973   88-4929
ISBN 0-398-05492-4

To Cheryl Suzanne Pahz
for her support, patience, and understanding

PREFACE

FOR MANY YEARS the number of families choosing to adopt from a country other than the United States has been increasing. Of that number, more and more families are deciding to adopt from Latin America.

This book is intended for prospective adoptive parents who are planning to adopt a child from Central or South America.

The volume is unique in adoption literature, being told from an AGENCY Perspective.

Adoption procedures, expectations and requirements are explained in great detail and always through the eyes of the agency professional.

The practical information is derived from the author's experience as Executive Director of Children's Hope Adoption Services, an international child-placing agency which specializes in adoptions from Latin America.

For anyone contemplating an adoption from Latin America, **Adopting From Latin America: An AGENCY Perspective,** should provide a valuable resource and an indispensable tool.

ACKNOWLEDGMENTS

I WOULD LIKE to express my appreciation to all those who have helped in any way to bring about this edition.

Firstly, I must thank Dr. Larry Rosser and his wife Gail who first located for us our daughter, Lisa, and by so doing introduced us to the world of international adoptions. I have often wondered if the doctor and his wife ever realized the amount of happiness and joy they brought our family by this singular act of kindness.

Reverend, Victor Estrada was instrumental in introducing me to the possibility of finding homes for orphaned children in Guatemala and initially developing the idea for Children's Hope Adoption Service.

Our adoption program has become successful only through the unselfish efforts of many people, both within and outside the United States. To our Latin American friends I would like to offer my gratitude; especially to Gloria Murga, Eddy and Elmer Dahlman, Lila and Guido Mass, Yadira Couart, and the many fine professionals we have been privileged to work with in various countries.

In the United States we have learned about adoptions through the efforts of our mentor and good friend, Annette O'Brien. In addition we have been fortunate to have an excellent staff of social workers, including: Chris Sloan, Carol Belland, Marsha Budd, Nancy Wilson and Deanna Heath. We owe much of our success to our translator, advisor, and friend, Mr. Carlos Alvarado.

I want to especially thank all of those who allowed me to reproduce their material from previous publications: Heino R. Erichsen of the Los Niños International Adoption Center, Nancy Cameron of LIMIAR U.S.A., Deborah McCurdy of the International Concerns Committee for Children, Dr. Jerri Ann Jenista, and Dr. Charles J. Zelnick. Certain organizations have also provided me with permission to reproduce their materials, including: International Adoptions Incorporated, The

National Committee for Adoption and *OURS: The Magazine for Adoptive Families*. The addition of this material greatly enhanced the quality of this enterprise.

Finally, for the technical assistance I received during the preparation of this manuscript, I would like to thank my cousin, Ms. Harriet Drucker, and my wife, Cheryl Pahz, for their assistance. Also, many thanks to the professional colleagues who took the time to review my manuscript and give me their thoughts and comments.

James A. Pahz

CONTENTS

ADOPTING
FROM
LATIN AMERICA

An AGENCY Perspective

CHAPTER ONE

INTRODUCTION

A WORD OF EXPLANATION—
WHAT IS AN AGENCY PERSPECTIVE?

MY WIFE and I have adopted two children from Latin America. For years, our perspective on adoption was as adoptive parents. We were never very active in parent groups, however, and only occasionally participated in such organizations. When we did, we heard talk of callous social workers (the "social work mentality") and how agencies were hard, bureaucratic entities that lacked sensitivity and heart.

One of the stories we heard concerned a family who received a referral for a child from overseas. The family had been waiting for a child for over one year and, naturally, they were excited. The social service worker called the family and informed them when she received a medical report and photographs of "their" child. The parents, couldn't wait to see the pictures of their new child, and asked if they could meet with the social worker immediately.

"Oh no," she replied, "I couldn't do that. I'm quite busy today and tomorrow is a holiday—I will bring the pictures to you next Monday."

This story was told to illustrate the insensitivity of the social worker and, at the same time, the long-suffering patience of the adoptive parents. Although I heard this story in one version or another on numerous occasions, I never questioned whether or not it was true; I simply accepted it on faith. I also accepted, perhaps without realizing so until now, that in the world of adoptions, there seemed to be "good guys" and "bad guys," with the adoptive parents always wearing the white hats.

Then something happened to alter my point of view. As time passed, more and more adoptive families requested assistance of my wife and me in pursuing their children's adoptions from overseas. Since we had friends in other countries as well as practical experience ourselves, some felt we were in a position to help.

In the fall of 1984, I was scheduled to take a sabbatical leave from Central Michigan University. It was known within our community that I would be traveling to Central America. I was contacted by a local parent group and asked, while on my travels, if I might "look around" and see whether or not children were available for adoption.

While in Central America I met with missionaries, priests, medical personnel and orphanage directors. I found that children were, in fact, available. Many of these people indicated they had previously worked with adoption programs in the United States but found the experience unsatisfactory. They saw North Americans as "pushy," "demanding," and wanting everything completed by yesterday. They were not interested in working with people in the United States again. I inquired whether they would work with me to facilitate adoptions if I could start a program when I returned to the United States. Of course, I promised **my program would be different.** We would not be pushy, etc. I received enough commitments so that when I did return I developed a proposal to start an agency in Michigan. The proposal was accepted, and in the summer of 1985 Children's Hope was born.

Directing an international adoption program was unlike anything I had previously done. I learned soon that I was no longer wearing the white hat. I was now on the other side of the fence and on that side people looked at me differently. Things were starting to look different to me also. As the agency dealt with more and more people and had success and failure, I developed what I now refer to as **"agency perspective."** Through this perspective I learned that there are two sides to every adoptive misunderstanding and when things go wrong it is not necessarily the agency's fault.

For example: it is not our fault if a birthmother changes her mind at the last minute and decides to keep her baby. This is within her rights and she is permitted to do this in every country in which we work.

It is not our fault if a baby in a foreign orphanage becomes sick and dies. It is one of the great misfortunes of life, but children sometimes become terminally ill.

It is not our fault if children come to the United States with undiagnosed medical problems, even though they already had an overseas examination and were reported healthy.

It is not our fault if a moratorium is placed on adoptions in a foreign country.

It is not our fault if a foreign government falls and/or adoptions are halted for political reasons.

It is not our fault if the people who run an overseas program change their mind about placing a child because they perceive an American family as not having enough money or enough time to spend with the child.

In short, though I realize it sounds defensive, it's not the agency's fault if any of these things go wrong which might delay or prevent someone from completing his or her adoption as rapidly as would be wished! They are things which are simply beyond the agency's control.

Yet, even though these things are not our fault, we have been blamed for every one of them! And, by being blamed and trying to offer our words of explanation and support, we began to look at adoptive parents in a different light. Certainly it was different than we saw ourselves when we were potential adoptive parents. You might say, we began to take on some of that "social work mentality" we had previously heard so much about.

We came to believe that not all prospective adoptive parents are praiseworthy, some are not even tolerable.

We began to feel it was not insensitive to use a telephone answering machine so that we could take adoption calls during business hours instead of during the middle of dinner.

We came to think it was necessary to impose adoption fees sufficient to meet agency expenses both overseas and at home.

We came to ask parents to pay in **advance of service,** after some had promised to pay, but subsequently never did.

We stopped taking requests from people who wanted **only** a newborn female, or a baby with **only** very light colored skin.

We required parents to sign a binding contract relieving the agency of liability if something **out-of-our-hands** went wrong.

We required parents to be **patient and reasonable.**

In short, we began to see ourselves as advocates primarily for the child and not the adoptive parents.

And after developing all these criteria, we began to screen applicants more carefully and accept as clients only those with whom we felt we could work.

THE DIFFICULTY
OF AN INTERNATIONAL ADOPTION

Adopting a child from Latin America is not usually an easy task. It can be, although it can frequently be difficult. It is our job as an agency to make it as easy for the parents as possible, while, at the same time, imparting to them the realities of the adoption experience and in particular that of Latin America.

Clients can be very demanding. Many times, clients come to Children's Hope with unrealistic expectations. If things don't go just the way they want, they expect a refund of their money or a promise that everything will work out. We even had one family threaten a lawsuit because in their mind a referral was not forthcoming as fast as they wanted. After a four-month wait for a referral their attorney wrote that the stress of the waiting experience was causing them "excessive emotional trauma" and we would have to inform them **exactly** when their child was coming or compensate them later for their "pain and suffering."

We try, right from the start, to explain to all applicants what they can expect in pursuing an adoption from Latin America. And for their sake as well as ours we carefully explain all of the risks involved so there can be no misunderstanding later.

We have discovered that one effective way to present the situation is by comparing the adoption process to the pursuit of a college degree. A college or university, we say, provides a service, not a product. When you are accepted there is no guarantee that you will pass your courses or even complete the academic program to get your degree. If you are successful and graduate, there is no promise that you will find a job in your chosen field or one that pays you what you think is enough money.

Most people understand that if you fail your courses, the college will not return your money. The school has provided the instruction and it is not their fault if you failed. Perhaps you didn't go to class or didn't study for your examinations. For whatever reason, the school has already paid the instructor his or her salary and they regard their obligation to you as finished.

If you graduate, yet can't find the job you think you are entitled to, again, the college or university does not refund your money. Their position would be "that's unfortunate, we tried our best, but we **never guaranteed** you would find the right job. All we said was with training and preparation you would be **more likely** to find it."

This, we explain, is like applying to an agency in pursuit of an international adoption; again, **there are no guarantees.** The agency, like the college or university, is performing a service. With their assistance you are **more likely to find the child** for which you are looking, but more likely is not absolutely. There are a lot of individuals involved — each of whom plays an important part. These "components" are interconnected much like the links in a chain — and (to continue the analogy) should any one of these links break, the chain is broken. Just plain luck also plays a part in the adoption experience.

When you apply to have your homestudy done, there is no guarantee that you will be approved. You are not buying a homestudy — they are not for sale. You are paying for a professional evaluation. By going to a licensed agency you are going to those whom the state has deemed qualified to render a professional judgement.

If the agency feels they cannot support your efforts at adoption you will be "disapproved." This does not entitle you to a refund. It's unfortunate, but the agency has done what it was contracted to do — provide the evaluation. That you didn't like or agree with their judgement is irrelevant.

After all of your adoption paperwork is completed and your dossier is overseas, almost anything can happen. Some things the agency has control over, some things they don't. In either case, the agency as well as the foreign child-placing entity will most likely put the interests of the child ahead of those of the waiting parents. The child is their primary concern. Because of such perspectives, agencies may not always do things the way an adoptive parent desires. This makes some people angry.

If the university has the responsibility to prepare students for the "real world," then the agency has the responsibility to prepare clients for the "reality of the international adoption experience." That reality is, **there simply are no guarantees. Absolute predictability does not exist in this realm.** If you decide you want to adopt from Latin America then do so with your eyes open. Understand that you are taking a gamble. You are pursuing this avenue as a mature adult and accepting the risks involved.

For most people the gamble pays off and they are rewarded with the object of their desire. It happened for my wife and me and for almost all of the clients who have been through the Children's Hope program during the last two years. However, most people doesn't mean everyone. You may lose all the money you send overseas. You may see your hopes dashed and you may be put under enormous stress. You need to know these things right from the start and it is the responsibility of any honest and ethical agency to inform you of these realities.

A HOW-TO-DO-IT VOLUME

Adopting From Latin America: An AGENCY Perspective is a "how to do it" volume. It is told from a somewhat different point of view than most texts on adoption. It is told from the point of view of the agency looking critically at the applicant; this is what we mean by "agency perspective."

There are adoption resource books told from the vantage point of the adopting parent, and those of the impartial observer, but I am not aware of one viewing the client from the angle we have chosen. By so doing, it is not meant to be an elitist point of view or to imply that our position is more valid than that of the adoptive parent; rather, I am attempting to show that there is another way of looking at things. As the saying goes, "There are two sides to every coin."

It is also hoped that this text will take some of the "mystery" out of adoption and adoption agencies. Although it is not always apparent or obvious to adopting parents, agencies really do want parents to succeed at their adoption efforts.

THE RELATIONSHIP OF THE CLIENT
TO THE AGENCY

There often occurs a love/hate relationship between parents and their agency. The parents feel vulnerable, not in control, and overawed when dealing with the agency and their worker. The agency appears to have complete control with the ability to grant or deny parents their greatest wish. At times, parents fear and resent this "power," yet feel unable to express their feelings due to fear of adverse consequences.

Most of this "power" is illusory. Agencies are not all that powerful. They cannot arbitrarily make decisions concerning families and are regulated by state licensing requirements and are subordinate to decisions by the courts. Agencies desperately want the parents to succeed at adopting; they have nothing to gain if the adoption fails. Most of the rules and requirements which parents view as annoying obstacles have not been invented by the agency. When an agency requires a form, homestudy, or a medical report, it is merely following rules by which it must abide to be in compliance with state and federal regulations.

Unfortunately, the agency is in the middle, trying to meet regulatory requirements set by government entities and attempting at the same time to assist parents. During this process, any frustrations, bureaucratic problems, delays or inconsistencies are attributed by parents to the agency. The agency becomes the "fall guy" and assumes responsibility for the entire system, with all its imperfections and inconsistencies. Agencies can do little to change the system because:

1. They don't have the time, resources, or influence.
2. Changing the system would be challenging the authority figures with whom the agency needs to have a good relationship to survive as an agency.
3. Though we can educate and inform legislators and the general public, it is not within the agency's purveyance to propose adoption legislation.

Since we started Children's Hope we have placed many children in adoptive homes. If there is one lesson we have learned by working with adoptive parents, it is that, as an agency, you are either loved or hated! If the process of adopting internationally works well, you receive many thankful letters, indicating the parents' appreciation. But when there is a setback or disaster, some parents, like the one's mentioned who did not get their referral quickly enough, head straight to the lawyer's office. Such behavior usually ensures that an agency will discontinue their professional relationship with the family. If parents really want a child, having their attorney threaten the agency with a lawsuit is not an intelligent strategy. Fortunately, we have not met many individuals who have resorted to this method, but we have met one or two!

For the purpose of simplicity we use Children's Hope as a model of an International Child-Placing Agency and describe OUR procedures for accomplishing adoptions. The reader must realize, however, that there are many international adoption programs in the United States, operating in many different countries, each with its own unique set of procedures. Children's Hope is merely one of many and when we mention it specifically, it is only for the sake of providing an example. Furthermore, Children's Hope works exclusively from Latin America. There are many distinct differences between adoptions from Latin America and those of Korea and India. For one thing, with Korea and India you deal with only one government (although each state in India may interpret the law differently). With Latin American countries there is a different government in each country (6 in Central America and 13 in South America), each with its own laws and regulations concerning adoption. Another significant difference between adoptions from Latin America and those from India or Korea is that with Latin American adoptions it is frequently necessary for the parents to travel overseas to get their child. They may complete and finalize the adoption overseas or they may receive a guardianship, but in either case, it is usually necessary to travel.

These are not the only differences, but they are probably the most important ones. You may need to use the services of interpreters to send your documents with Spanish translations. When sending your documents you will most likely use a courier service. Also, documents for Latin America must go through a "legalization" process in the U.S. before acceptance in a foreign court. These inconveniences, although annoying, can be overcome, however, by anyone who truly wants a child. In Latin America, adoption is not something that just happens while you wait here in the U.S. — it is an experience in which you are vitally involved. Like natural childbirth, you know what's happening throughout the whole process — you are contributing to the event — and you will remember it in vivid detail for the rest of your life!

We hope you find this edition useful. If it provides you with information you need to initiate and accomplish a successful overseas adoption, or if it enables you to better work with your agency, then we have achieved our purpose.

A FEW WORDS ON TERMINOLOGY

In the language of adoption, there are many words which can be misleading. Also, there are different ways of writing one word to illustrate a concept. For example, the written evaluation of the capacity for parenthood is usually referred to as a "homestudy" or "home-study" or "home study." None of these three ways of writing this word are incorrect; it's a matter of preference. You will see each of them used. We prefer to use "homestudy" as one word, since it is the process of evaluating a family and not simply studying the home. That is our personal preference. Actually, a more accurate though somewhat cumbersome phrase, would be "adoption-readiness study."
Other words for single concepts include:

International Adoption/Intercountry Adoption — currently "Intercountry Adoption" is the more popular term, however we use "International Adoption" more frequently because we like the sound of it and are more familiar with it — but we also use "Intercountry Adoption."

Social Service Worker/Social Worker/Case Worker — these terms all refer to the individual assigned to work with the adoptive family and conduct the homestudy. The person has this job title because of the job activity as well as his/her educational achievement. Usually such an individual has received a Bachelor (or Master's) Degree in Social Work. These individuals must meet their state's licensing criteria to be eligible for such a position.

Prospective Parents/Adoptive Parents/Parents (not to exclude single parent)/ Family/Couple/Parent — though technically different these terms are frequently used interchangeably to refer to the individuals seeking to adopt the child.

Direct Adoption/Independent Adoption/Parent-Initiated Adoption — all refer to the process of locating a child overseas by the parents themselves and then being responsible themselves for completing the paperwork and legalities with a minimum of agency involvement. (A licensed agency or independent licensed social worker will still be required to conduct a homestudy. This is an Immigration requirement so that the adopted child can obtain a visa to enter the U.S.).

Birth-Mother/Birthmother/Biological Mother/First Mother/Real Mother — these are used interchangeably. The only objectionable term is "real mother" and it should be avoided. A child's *real* mother is obviously the individual who has nurtured (mothered) that child during his/her childhood. Referring to a birthmother as the real mother is offensive to most adoptive parents, and justifiably so.

If there is more than one term and one is **highlighted,** that is our preferred term. A more extensive listing of terminology will be found in the appendix section on **Adoption Terminology.**

CHAPTER TWO

BUILDING FAMILIES
THROUGH INTERNATIONAL ADOPTION*

International (Intercountry) Adoption Defined

INTERNATIONAL (or intercountry) adoption refers to the process by which a married couple or single adult adopts a child from a country other than their own.

ADDING TO YOUR FAMILY
THROUGH INTERNATIONAL ADOPTION
ONE WAY OF LOOKING AT THINGS

Approximately one in every six couples in the United States today suffers from infertility. Infertility is defined medically as the inability to conceive after trying for a period of one year. Medical technology may help about half of these couples, but approximately five million individuals will remain infertile after all available medical treatment has been rendered. For persons in this group who desire the parenting experience, adoption is often the most promising solution.

In the United States today, the actual process of adopting a child is seldom what prospective parents expect. It is frequently frustrating and fraught with disappointment. The National Committee for Adoption, an organization composed of more than 130 member adoption agencies, estimates that for the 25,000 babies available for adoption annually, there are approximately two million couples waiting to adopt children.

---

*Much of the material in Chapter Two originally appeared in an article "Building Families Through International Adoption," published in Volume 8, Number 1, of *International Quarterly of Community Health Education.* The material is reproduced through the courtesy of Baywood Publishing Company, Inc., copyright 1987, Baywood Publishing Co., Inc.

When couples are told the sobering statistics, and that they can expect to wait seven years or more before finding their child, they look elsewhere—and elsewhere there are children. For many reasons, in other countries, there are children needing families. These children are homeless because of natural disaster, war, or extreme poverty . . . but most often they simply are the offspring of single, working women who cannot afford to care for them properly. Such women voluntarily relinquish their children for adoption, hoping this will ensure a brighter future for their child than would otherwise be possible. It is an act of unselfish love which motivates such women, and they benefit only by knowing their child will have the opportunity for a happy, more promising life.

The process of matching these children with parents who wish to adopt them is what **"international or intercountry" adoption** is about. It refers to the method by which a married couple or single adult adopts a child from a country other than their own. In the United States during the last twenty-five years, intercountry adoptions have become increasingly common. While in 1979 there were 4,864 foreign children adopted, in 1984 there were 8,327 and in 1985 there were 9,286. Most of these were infants and toddlers who came from Asia and Latin America.[1]

International adoption is not simple, and adoptions from Latin America are the most difficult of all! More often than not it is a frustrating experience. Disappointment, delays and high cost are common. Foreign government regulations change frequently and foreign governments change occasionally. Yet, in the end, for most families it is worth the effort. Though the experience may be harrowing, it is a nightmare worth having since it makes possible that special child—a unique individual for whom one has waited so long! For many couples this is the only way they can ever become a family.

A HISTORICAL PERSPECTIVE—
ANOTHER WAY OF LOOKING AT THINGS

International Adoption became a widespread practice following the conclusion of World War II. As a natural consequence of war, there were

---

1. National Committee for Adoption, *Adoption Factbook; United States Data, Issues, Regulations and Resources* (Washington, D.C.: National Committee for Adoption, 1985), pp. 122-123.

large numbers of orphaned and abandoned children in need of permanent, loving homes. These children traveled from one European country to another or to the United States or Canada until they were eventually settled with new families. Since then, adoption across geopolitical lines has increased with ever greater frequency.[2]

The character of international adoption has changed during the last forty years. Now it is not so much a matter of having too many orphaned children in need of families, but rather of having **too many families who want children!** In the more affluent and technologically developed countries, infertility is a significant problem. In these same countries there are fewer and fewer available children. This increasingly difficult situation dictates that couples wishing to adopt children turn their attention overseas.[3]

For the last thirty years or so, Asia — and in particular Korea — was the main source of such children. Though Korea continues to be a primary source, adoptions from Korea are declining in number. More and more international adoptions are coming from Latin America.[4]

For the Latin American countries, international adoption represents a relatively new phenomenon. As a social issue it is one which Latin American governments have constantly had to grapple with. Although the subject of international adoption was previously covered in two historic documents, the Bustamante Code of 1928 and the Montevideo Treaty of 1940, these documents are now old and have little relevance to international adoption as practiced today.[5]

ISSUES OF ADOPTION AND CONCERNS OF THE COUNTRIES INVOLVED

From the perspective of the Latin American governments, international adoption is regarded with disfavor. The press continuously rails against abuses of the process with stories of unscrupulous entrepreneurs getting rich through the "sale" of children. Such stories frequently include dramatic photographs of crying orphans left in deplorable conditions (see Chapter 3, *Adoption and Scandal*). Some of the most recent

---

2. Francisco J. Pilotti, "Intercountry Adoption: A View From Latin America," *Child Welfare: Journal of the Child Welfare League of America*, LXIV, No. 1 (1985), 26.

3. National Committee for Adoption, pp. 28-29.

4. Ibid., pp. 122-123.

5. Pilotti, p. 32.

stories regarding adoption involve the sale of healthy infants to individuals for the purpose of transplanting the babies' organs into unhealthy infants overseas! Another rumor is that infants are bought by drug dealers who will then stuff the bodies with illicit drugs. The dead infants are then used to smuggle the drugs into various countries. Such stories can be successful tools for political manipulations—and they also help sell newspapers.[6,7]

With such propaganda, it is little wonder that many regard the practice of international adoption with suspicion and hostility. However, newspapers alone are not responsible for the distaste many Latin Americans feel toward international adoption. A country, any country, does not want to appear to the rest of the world as unable to take care of its own children. Even orphaned and abandoned children represent a resource for the future.

Also, there is the very real issue of exploitation of third world countries by the people from more affluent societies. Although adoption agencies constantly proclaim that no money is given to induce young, poor, urban women to relinquish their offspring, the reality is often quite different. Agencies in the United States and Europe can only be partially held responsible for the disreputable behavior of their representatives in countries so distant. Everyone knows there are "baby brokers," as well as attorneys and others who willingly capitalize on situations where the interests of a wealthy individual in a developed country contrast with those of an impoverished birthmother. There is desperation on both sides; on the one, the potential parents so desperately want to experience parenthood and, on the other, the individual needs merely to survive!

THE ETHICS OF
U.S. BASED ADOPTION PROGRAMS OVERSEAS
IN ESTABLISHING ADOPTION SOURCES

This writer has been to Latin America five times during the last two years. On every trip, while staying at a major hotel, I encountered agency personnel in search of "contacts" or "new sources" for adoptable

---

6. Heino Erichsen, "International Adoption and the Media," *Newsletter of the Los Ninos Adoption Center,* March 1987, pp. 1-3.

7. Nancy Cameron, "A View From the Other Side," *OURS: The Magazine of Adoptive Families,* December 1986, p. 6.

children. Such people came from new as well as established and well-known adoption programs. What they had in common was an almost missionary zeal as they went about their business of "hustling up" adoptable children. It was like an Agency Easter Egg Hunt—each director collecting the adoptable children while they formed new relationships with attorneys and adoption facilitators. In their exuberance at finding such "sources," they frequently overlooked the potential for harm such hastily formed liaisons can bring. This writer believes there are important ethical and human value questions that are being ignored by some U.S.-based international adoption programs. Unquestionably, many of these contacts will be with individuals who want only to profit financially from adoptions. What they will do in their pursuit of children, after the agency director returns home, might be illegal. Inevitably, some waiting family in the United States will suffer the consequences of such arrangements. The behavior of the representatives of these U.S. programs does not go unnoticed by the native citizenry. Such actions do nothing to better the image of international adoption. It only serves to reinforce the negative perceptions already held by most Latin Americans.

There is considerable opinion in those countries that the role of adoption agencies is to find and remove "the best" children. The International Concerns Committee for Children (Boulder, Colorado) has tried to educate U.S. agencies to their responsibility in foreign countries. Besides adoption, such agencies should develop programs for "unadoptable" children (be they unadoptable because of age, medical problems, or the existence of a relative keeping them in legal limbo).

Such programs are currently maintained by many reputable international child-placing programs, including: Covenants Children in Latin America; PACT (Partners Aiding Children Today), Americans for International Aid and Adoption, Holt International Children's Services, Adoption Services of WACAP (Povedorio Project), Open Arms, International Mission of Hope (Asha Kendra) in India, and others. Some countries, such as India, will not permit an agency to be licensed to do **only** adoptions; they must also have some other child welfare activity.

Ethical and human value aspects of international adoption programs need to be investigated and studied carefully in the future. Standards of behavior need to be developed and programs need to be more concerned with the image they are fostering. Efforts at self-regulation through such organizations as those of the **Joint Council on International Children's Services From North America** should be applauded. Programs like the **International Concerns Committee for Children** serve a useful function in monitoring overseas efforts and reporting their observations in their annual *Report on Foreign Adoption*. It goes without saying that if U.S.-based international adoption programs continue to behave poorly there will soon be some regulatory body that will step in and establish rigid guidelines concerning what is and is not permissible. That can only serve to make international adoption more difficult than it already is.

Then too, it is not just agencies which are to blame. Parents' also share some of the fault for the "take the child and run" philosophy. After the child is home, many parents no longer give donations, assist agencies in providing periodic reports, help with adoption legislation, or publicize bad agency practice. Since their child is **already here,** they feel their responsibility is finished.

THE INTERNATIONAL ADOPTION SCENE TODAY

The international adoption scene has been and continues to be ripe for abuse. It is no wonder the subject is controversial.

Because of a combination of all the previously listed factors, some governments, like Colombia, have legislated that all adoptions proceed through a government agency. Not only does this eliminate much of what can go wrong with adoptions, it also keeps the cost reasonable in comparison with other Latin American countries. The Bienestar organization (the government social welfare program) charges no program fees for adoption and the couple can expect to pay standard legal expenses and translation fees. Though working through a bureaucracy makes the adoption more cumbersome and slower, it removes the profit incentive from private attorneys and baby-brokers and makes the process safer for the adopting family.

Before initiating this system, Colombia, like most other Latin American countries, had many adoption scandals. The new system has been hailed as a model for other countries and efforts have been made to emulate it. Naturally it is opposed by some private attorneys who see intercountry adoption as a lucrative part of their business.

This is not to imply that adoptions through private attorneys are illegal or exploitative. Many attorneys are reputable and provide a good service for both birthmothers and families. However, it is often difficult to sort the reputable ones from the disreputable.

Some states including, Connecticut, Delaware, Massachusetts, Michigan and Minnesota, prohibit attorney-mediated or "private" adoption. There are good reasons for this including, including:

1. Who will be responsible for providing counseling to a woman thinking of relinquishing her child?

2. Who will be responsible for the child if something goes wrong after the child is relinquished, but before the adoptive parents take a legal guardianship? What will happen if the child is born retarded, has serious disease, or some other unfortunate situation? Who represents the child's interests?

3. What happens if the adoption is not successful? Who is going to be responsible for finding a second adoptive family for the child? Again, who will represent the child's interest?

4. If it turns out that the adoption was a "gray" or "black" market adoption, i.e., an illegal adoption, who will protect the rights of the parents? Who will be responsible for reimbursing them for money expended toward the adoption. Who will protect such parents against prosecution if it is thought they willingly conspired in this illegal enterprise? And again, who will protect the rights of this child in such a situation, when that child may be removed from the adoptive home and returned to his place of origin? The tragic case of the adopted Steinberg children, one beaten to death and the other left tied to a chair, as reported in the national media in November of 1987, is an illustration of why private adoptions have been eliminated in many states.

Such laws which prohibit private adoptions are not passed without a great deal of thought and testimony from knowledgeable experts. Parents need know the adoption laws and understand they were passed for the protection of the interests of the child and parents. They are meant to protect both from the abuses in the adoption system. It should be clear, that abuses are not just a domestic problem. Abuses can occur with equal or greater frequency with international adoptions. With this in mind, some parents may choose for ethical reasons not to work with any private attorney.

At the time of this writing, intercountry adoption continues to be an emotional and controversial issue throughout Latin America. What the future holds is uncertain, though changes in overseas regulations are likely.

Whether you look at international adoption as a blessing or shame largely depends on your perspective. From the eyes of the potential parent it is a wonderful thing. Yet, viewed from the prospective of the Latin American official, it is a practice questionable at best and one not to be encouraged.

MORE LATIN AMERICANS ARE THEMSELVES ADOPTING

Traditionally, when Latin Americans wanted to adopt, the process had been secretive and hidden. Parents of upper class status would adopt children from a lower class family. However they would not want it known that their children were of an *inferior* status or that they themselves were infertile. Consequently, they would register the birth of the adopted child as their own and no questions would be asked. It is still possible to do this in many Latin American countries, but it is becoming less and less necessary. Fortunately, times are changing. The stigma of adoption in the last two decades has diminished significantly. It is well known that other people (Americans, Europeans, Scandinavians) put a great value on the "unwanted" children of Latin America. As time passes, the process of adoption by Latins is gaining social acceptance. Editorials in almost every Latin American country proclaim how citizens of their country should be given preference in adopting children (rather than sending the children overseas). Obviously, if such a trend continues, it will lessen the number of orphans available for adoption by North Americans.

CHAPTER THREE

ADOPTION AND SCANDAL

ADOPTION AS SEEN BY THE PRESS — A TOUGH LESSON LEARNED

INTERNATIONAL ADOPTION and scandal seem to go hand-in-hand. At Children's Hope we receive a steady stream of newspaper clippings regarding various adoption schemes which are sent to us by concerned parents. Most are about people or programs placing babies from foreign countries for exorbitant sums of money. In many stories, the babies are not legitimate orphans, but have been procured from birthmothers through deceit, coercive threat, or promise of a large sum of money.

When one reads the newspapers, the general assumption is that the material you are reading is true. At Children's Hope we have learned through our own experience, however, that this assumption is often false. There is nothing like a juicy scandal to send newspaper sales soaring and adoption controversy makes exciting reading.

This point was brought home to us over the Christmas holidays in 1986 when our contractual worker and her retired husband, residing in Guatemala City, were arrested for "stealing and selling babies" to rich Americans. Here is the story, as reported in the December 23 edition of the newspaper, *La Hora*.

> The North American Severino Goularth Silva, 74 years old, from Massachusetts, was detained by the National Police Force along with his wife Maria Magdalena Morales Rojas de Silva, 43 years old, because they had a business consisting of the trafficking of children, an activity they have performed for several years, according to information by the police.
>
> The authorities were able to discover the business by means of a search they performed in a house on First Street . . . where they found

two minors that were already sold and would have soon been sent to the United States. Also in the same residence were two young girls who were in charge of feeding the minors who were to be sold: these two girls said that the business has gone on for some time. They were in a position to know, since they cared for the babies from the time they were taken to the house until they were taken out of the country.

The baby girls rescued by the police are Adys Lin Telon, 2 months old, daughter of Rosa Telon, a neighbor on First Street and Claudia Liseth Lopez, daughter of Ana Cecilia Lopez. Both women indicated to the police that their daughters had been kidnapped and currently are the plaintiffs of the two people detained for holding and trafficking of minors. Meanwhile, the two minors were sent to the Children's House of Old Guatemala, where they are being cared for until the police locate their mothers.

Official police sources indicate that the detained North American, along with his wife, are being subjected to a minutely cautious investigation since there is already evidence that they have sold numerous minors, for whom they obtained prices which fluctuated between one hundred and fifty thousand dollars and three hundred thousand dollars, depending on the economic capacity of the adopting parents of the minors, who were sent to foreign countries.

Police authorities pointed out that the two people detained are accused of the crime of abducting minors, because there are concrete denunciations that the baby girls, as with the other minors who were sold, were abducted by women who then took them (the children) to the house on First Street, which was searched via the warrant issued by the sixth judge of Criminal Justice . . .

Now, here is a chilling story which indicates a very real crime had been committed, even if the story does contain inconsistencies — for example, the mothers of the infants are the plaintiffs of the case, but the police are trying to locate the mothers to return their babies to them (?). However, **since we were involved** in this particular situation, we know first hand how much misinformation had been passed on as "fact" when it was presented in printed form.

Here is what really happened. Both women had on their own volition approached the Children's Hope representative and inquired about releasing their babies (who were not yet born) for adoption. One woman was employed and felt she couldn't financially afford another child and the second was a fifteen-year-old girl who was herself still in school. They requested only that their medical expenses be paid and that they would surrender their babies for adoption. Both later delivered their babies and released them as planned. The mothers had already made a court declaration and the babies were in legitimate foster care.

Someone (it has never been determined who) reported to the police that the woman who worked for Children's Hope was making large amounts of money, selling babies to "rich North Americans." The police arrived late in the afternoon and demanded to see the documentation on the children. Our worker indicated the lawyer kept the legal documents in her office. The lawyer was out of town on Christmas vacation. When the lawyer could not be reached, the police arrested all the adult occupants. This event occurred immediately before Christmas and the judge was also on Christmas vacation. A hearing to set bail could not be held until the judge returned to court, which was ten days away. The woman and her husband, therefore, had to remain in a Guatemalan prison until court could be convened and bail arranged. It was presumed the defendants were guilty and the burden of proof was on the defendants to show they were innocent.

When we at Children's Hope learned of this incident, the Director flew to Guatemala to provide information about the adoption program. The charges against the woman and her husband were subsequently dismissed. Both birthmothers testified in court they had freely given their babies for adoption and had not received any money. Only their medical expenses had been paid. There were, of course, no outrageous fees received by our representatives. **The experience taught us to regard newspaper accounts on adoption scandals with a great deal of skepticism!**

The way the media reports on adoption matters was described nicely in an article in the *Los Ninos News*. The article was written by **Heino R. Erichsen** and appeared in the March 1987 edition. Excerpts reproduced here by permission of the author:

International Adoption and the Media
by Heino R. Erichsen

Because adoption has not been openly practiced in Latin America or in other Third World countries, international adoption is not understood by vast segments of the population. Very little educational material is dispersed on the positive aspects of adoption. And, Latin American couples who adopt are often secretive about it.

Babies of the lowest socio-economic classes usually are the ones adopted; infertile couples of the upper socio-economic classes are usually the ones who adopt. Because infertility in Latin America is still considered shameful, many couples still pretend that the child was born to them. Adoptions by nationals in their own country often is no more than registration of the adoptive parents' names on the child's birth certificate without the court process. Not only does this method assure privacy, it is also faster and less expensive. U.S. citizens cannot use this method.

Not all Latin American couples are comfortable with adopting children of low class parentage, however. Los Ninos International, as well as other private agencies, receive calls and letters from Mexican and Colombian prospective adoptive parents who wish to adopt a white American baby, since in their minds it will raise, rather than lower, their social status. Since we already have U.S. citizens prepared for adoption, we have to turn them down.

These couples may or may not have tried another option: fertility clinics that co-exist in the same cities as abandoned street children. When we were in Colombia in 1973, we met a Colombian who sent his American-born wife to one of these clinics because he could not consider adopting "riff-raff." He had grown up in the slums, abandoned by his father. Through a combination of brains, determination, and luck, he acquired an education and an excellent job with the government. He believed the negative articles on adoption and held a fatalistic attitude toward the abandoned children.

Nevertheless, according to statistics, adoption is slowly gaining acceptance in the Latin American countries such as Colombia, Costa Rica, and Chile. While there are no data to prove it, I wonder if adoptions by U.S. citizens and Western Europeans have made Latin American orphans more socially acceptable. Occasionally, the media does a story on one of these couples, stressing how noble the couple is, and how lucky the child.

But, will the day ever come when there are more prospective Latin American adoptive parents than available babies? Given the high rate of population growth, it seems unlikely. And this is probably one of the reasons why the government welfare departments in most Latin American countries accept international adoption. Trouble begins in interpreting laws and procedures written for domestic adoptions in order to apply them to foreign adoptions. Exceptions occur in countries which have residency requirements for foreign adoptive parents.

Another source of bad press are foster homes. Most countries do not have laws or regulations governing the licensing of foster homes for children during the process of adoption or guardianship. There is often a conflict between the legal (court) process and the regulations of the welfare department (who may be called Bienestar, Patronato, SENAME, or so on). The entire legal process can be followed to the letter, yet the welfare department may intervene if someone brings to their attention the fact that at a certain address a number of children are being cared for. These places are often referred to as *casa gordas* (fattening-up houses) by the media. They do not understand that, in actuality, the children are being treated for malnutrition and parasites for which they never had attention previously.

An alternative has been to leave children with their birth mothers during the adoption or guardianship process. This is not the best solution if she lives in squalor, works outside of the home, or has other children to look after. The media and welfare departments in some countries even object to care provided for birth mothers during the later stages of pregnancy. In the U.S., maternity homes and foster homes are an accepted way of providing healthful conditions to the birth mother and the unborn child. In other countries, sheltering birth mothers may be construed as coercion even if the birth mother can exercise her universal right to release or to keep her offspring.

Every country has made news, at some time or other, regarding baby selling scandals, or other devious schemes. In response, the licensed agencies are investigated along with the racketeers. In countries where there are no licensing of adoption agencies, only lawyers can handle adoptions. Some of them quickly figured out that international adoption is the most lucrative kind of case. For example, when we started coordinating adoptions in Honduras four years ago, only three lawyers handled adoptions. Today, 80 lawyers do. Yet, few of them have tried to educate the general public about the benefits of adoption. Crude stories are generated by Honduran citizens who resent U.S. aid. Americans are reported to import children for organ transplants and child pornography.

Anyone who has or who is undergoing the multi-tiered process of the homestudy, immigration clearance (including FBI clearance), and the investigation of their documents overseas knows better. Prospective adopters of foreign children undergo more scrutiny than adopters of domestic children.

Our Guatemalan visitors brought news articles with them, which were in response to previously printed horror stories in Guatemalan papers. Allegations of kidnapping and medical experiments by U.S. citizens were repudiated by none less than the U.S. Embassy. The embassy official stated the conditions and safeguards were practiced by U.S. adoption agencies and by the U.S. Immigration and Naturalization Service. And, a minister of the Guatemalan government said that the allegations sounded like something out of a novel, rather than a newspaper. He added that reforms of some regulations are needed, however. One article brought to us ended with a statistic of 100,000 orphans created in Guatemala by their last period of violence.

Far from being discouraged by these problems, LNI is developing more and more programs with legal child-placing entities rather than with foreign lawyers and is participating in the establishment of foundations in countries where this is possible. . . .

One of the worst scandals, involving kidnapping and switching live babies of newly delivered mothers with deceased babies, was masterminded by a lawyer formerly on the staff of the Colombian welfare department. That year, adoptions came to a virtual halt as each case, through private and public agencies, as well as through lawyers, was investigated. Individual lawyers can no longer handle adoptions. The Colombian-born novelist, Gabriel Garcia Marquez, added fuel to the fire by claiming that North Americans were "importing babies like bags of coffee in order to obtain welfare benefits." At that time, we fired off a letter to his news-paper explaining the FBI clearance, I-600A and I-600 Petitions, as well as the orphan investigation conducted by the U.S. Consular Section abroad. Predictably, we did not receive a response. . . .

Recently, in an article about a contested surrogate case, a U.S. news magazine predicted that in the near future, "U.S. career-oriented couples would rent the wombs of Third World women." This proves that U.S. reporters do not research their articles very carefully, either. Would the U.S. Immigration and Naturalization service confer orphan status on a baby with three parents?

THE PERCEPTION OF ADOPTION IN FOREIGN COUNTRIES

We have already commented on the negative way that adoption is perceived in other countries in Chapter 2 and will expand on the topic with an article by Nancy Cameron reproduced in Chapter 6. It is regarded by many as a less than honorable practice. There appears to be a degree of collective shame when a society exports its children for adoption, even if those children are unwanted at home. Unspoken is the idea that the children are going to a life the adults covet and would gladly take for themselves if possible. North Americans are frequently regarded as rich, pushy, and demanding; they all drive two Cadillacs and can afford to pay a lot more money to get what they want. By Latin American standards North Americans are wealthy — but certainly not to the extent imagined by most Latin Americans.

For many attorneys, adoption is a profitable business. Some are baby brokers as well as lawyers and know the price the market will bear. Though a "finder's fee" is illegal in almost every country, many attorneys provide a "little something" to the woman who places her baby for adoption. The lawyers will then go to the adoption agency or adopting couple directly and request a price of several thousand dollars as "the legitimate adoption expenses" they incur. The adoptive parents have no choice but to meet these expenses or go elsewhere.

WORKING WITH OVERSEAS ATTORNEYS

When evaluating the most difficult adoptions that Children's Hope has been connected with in Latin America, we can, in every case, say they were troublesome because the professionals we depended upon for assistance were unprofessional by American standards.

In Guatemala we used the services of a "highly respected" attorney who had also served temporarily as a judge in the Court of Minors. This woman worked so slowly that another lawyer we use completed five adoptions in the time she could finish one! The unfortunate family involved in the adoption waited approximately one year for the conclusion of a process that should have taken three months. The attorney would not permit another lawyer to take over her case, as we requested, indicating that any other attorney "probably would be dishonest." She kept reminding us of her reputation and the need for caution in matters of adoption. She was **SO** cautious that the baby, languishing in the care of the government orphanage, eventually died. The attorney did not bother to inform Children's Hope about this tragedy; we had to learn it indirectly from others.

While our "respected" attorney plodded along in Guatemala, we had similar problems in Honduras. Again, we had a lawyer who seemed incapable of getting anything accomplished. When families went to the Honduran authorities to inquire about the status of their documents, the clerk would ask the family for the name of their lawyer. When they revealed his name, the clerk would reply, "Oh, he is your lawyer . . . (then the clerk would laugh). You will never get out of here!"

Distraught at hearing such words, one of our representatives went to see this attorney and was sexually assaulted by the lawyer! Complaints were later lodged against this individual in an attempt to have him discontinued from doing adoptions. At the time of this writing he is still assisting with adoption work for North American families.

What recourse does an adoptive parent or agency have in such situations—very little. The obvious answer is litigation. Both families could have mounted a reasonable malpractice suit against these so called "professionals," for such unprofessional behavior. Litigation, however, as a solution is not very practical. The adoptive parent is in a foreign country, it is expensive to remain there, they don't speak the language and a lawsuit takes a long time.

The very least agencies should do in such matters is report the offending lawyer to the court, the Department of Social Services of the country involved and the U.S. Embassy. If such actions are not done, such people will continue merrily along. Practical or not, if someone does not take the initiative to get rid of these individuals, the restrictive policies everybody fears will eventually go into effect, increasing the difficulty of adopting from overseas.

In addition, agencies should try to steer adoptive parents away from such individuals. Believing that prevention is easier than dealing with the problems later, Children's Hope now keeps a record of overseas attorneys and resource people engaged in adoption activities. We list those we have found to be cooperative and competent as well as those with whom we have had problems. We believe it is important to enable parents to avoid becoming involved with the unscrupulous, dishonest, or inept. We provide information to any adoptive family concerning our past experience with an individual. We do not, however, make a formal recommendation to parents whether or not to work with a particular individual. In addition, we advise parents to obtain information from the Latin American Parents Association which provides "fact sheets" concerning specific countries.

Reputation is no guarantee, but sometimes it is all a parent has to go on. In adoption, a good name is important. We try to encourage parents to work with persons of good reputation (it does not always work, but most of the time it does). We are especially wary of those attorneys who ask for **ALL** of their fees in advance, though it is reasonable to pay a portion in advance to cover the initial adoption expenses and foster care for the child. If the attorney is demanding complete payment up front, a parent probably can find another lawyer who will be willing to begin the work for a reasonable deposit and have the remainder paid after he/she renders professional services.

HOW TO AVOID
BECOMING INVOLVED IN A SCANDAL
OR OTHER PROBLEMATIC ADOPTION

1. Work through a licensed agency or well respected liaison organization.
2. Avoid unlicensed "facilitators" who claim to know someone overseas who can get you a baby, unless you personally know the facilitator and are confident the person's claims are true. Realize by pursuing this avenue you are increasing the risk that something can go wrong.
3. Don't work directly with an overseas attorney unless you personally know him/her or they have been recommended by people you know and trust.
4. Don't pay all your money in advance.

5. Don't agree to pay exorbitant fees. Check with your agency, parent support group or other knowledgable body to determine what fees are "reasonable."

6. Don't agree to pay additional expenses to the birthmother or her family. Don't promise to "help out" her unfortunate family.

7. Ask for references from U.S. families with children already placed.

8. Check out the source with the U.S. embassy in that country.

9. Write to the Department of Social Services of that country or the Juvenile Court and ask about the person.

CHAPTER FOUR

FORM AND STRUCTURE

TYPES OF INTERNATIONAL ADOPTION

INTERNATIONAL adoptions are basically of two types, although variations may occur. These are either (1) Agency Adoption, or (2) Parent-Initiated Adoption. Regardless of which type a parent pursues, he/she will be involved in bureaucracies of both the child's birth country and the United States. One of the largest and most complicated of these entities is the U.S. Immigration and Naturalization Service.

THE IMMIGRATION AND NATIONALITY ACT

As amended, The United States Immigration and Nationality Act of 1952, concerns the requirements for visa issuance for orphans entering the United States for the purpose of adoption. Such children may qualify as immediate relatives and may thus enter the country if: the adoptive family has met all **preadoptive requirements** of their state of residence or the parents have personally seen the child prior to or during the adoption process abroad.[1]

LEGAL AUTHORITY
FOR GRANTING IMMIGRANT STATUS

Section 101 of the Immigration and Nationality Act concerns itself with foreign born orphans who have been adopted or are being adopted

---

1. Title 8, U.S.C., Aliens and Nationality.

by American citizens. Through the provisions of this act, such children may receive the visa classification of an "immediate relative." The classification for orphans adopted abroad is an IR-3 and the classification for those children entering the U.S. for the purpose of adoption is an IR-4.

The definition of an "orphan," according to this law is a child under sixteen years of age, whose parents are deceased, or have abandoned the child, or have simply disappeared. An "orphan" may also result from a single parent who has irrevocably released the child for adoption. This is somewhat confusing. If there are no known parents, or if there is one known parent, who has released the child for adoption, that child is considered an orphan. However, under this definition, **if there are two known parents, the child cannot qualify as an orphan unless the child has been declared abandoned by the court.**

The law provides, that "Any citizen of the United States claiming that an alien is entitled to a preference status by reason of the relationship . . . may file a petition with the Attorney General for such classification."[2]

The **"Petition to Classify Orphan as an Immediate Relative,"** is known as an **I-600 petition.** This is a very important document and is absolutely necessary in an international adoption. The petition is filed with the Immigration and Naturalization Service. The Service has offices throughout the United States (Appendix D). Along with the petition parents must submit supporting documents and pay a filing fee of fifty dollars.

The law states that with respect to approval of the petition **"no petition may be approved on behalf of a child defined in Section 101 (b) (1) (F) unless a valid homestudy has been favorably recommended by an agency of the state of the child's proposed residence,** or, in the case of a child adopted abroad, by an appropriate public or private adoption agency which is licensed in the United States."[3]

---

2. 8 U.S.C. 1154, Sec. 204.

3. Sect. e. Even when a non-preference visa is applied for, the government requires an approved homestudy (sect. 208 (a) (8). The only instance when a child brought to the United States does not need to have a homestudy approved is when the child has remained in the physical and legal custody of his/her adoptive parents for a period of more than two years. Such a situation might occur with a missionary or military family who have lived in the country for some time and decide to adopt a child which has been living with the family.

In addition to an approved homestudy, the INS will want to see other documents in support of the I-600 Petition. An applicant will need to submit:

- Proof of U.S. citizenship
- Proof of marriage and/or proof of divorce
- Fingerprints (Form FD-258)
- Proof of financial ability (Affidavit of Support, Form I-134 and supporting documents)

The fingerprint charts can be prepared at a local INS office or at the police station in your community. It is very important to make sure the prints are clear—smudged charts will require that the entire procedure be repeated, which can cause interminable delays. It can take up to sixty days or more for a fingerprint check to be completed after fingerprints are sent to Washington by the local INS office.

In addition to these documents, an applicant will need to show the child's documents in order to get I-600 approval. These must be submitted in English, so if the original documents are in a foreign language they must be translated. After the adoption or guardianship has been completed overseas, the prospective parent or an agent of the parent (lawyer or agency representative) takes the following documents to the American Embassy in the country in which the adoption has taken place:

- Child's birth certificate
- Certified copy of adoption decree and translated copies of court documents
- Evidence that preadoptive requirements have been completed if child is to be adopted in the United States (guardianship cases)
- Release of parental responsibility signed by biological parent indicating inability to care for child
- Evidence of unconditional abandonment if child has been placed in an orphanage

An I-600 form must be approved for each child one wishes to adopt. A child cannot get permission to enter the United States until the I-600 petition has been approved.

Can you do anything to hasten the processing of the paperwork, even though you haven't yet located your child?

Yes, the INS has provided for this contingency by allowing prospective parents to file an **"Application for Advance Processing of Orphan**

Petition" (I-600A form) before their child is located. Thus the prospective parents can submit **SOME** of the materials INS will need to review in advance of actually locating the child abroad. The INS then makes a "preapproval" of the adoptive parents so all that will be necessary later is to review documents pertaining to the child. Once you locate your child and receive the child's documents you submit them to the INS with the "Petition to Classify Orphan as an Immediate Relative" (I-600 form) and "Affidavit of Support" form. Since you have already been "preapproved," it won't be necessary to resubmit the material you sent with the I-600A and you will not be required to pay an additional filing fee.

The main advantage of filing an I-600A (Application for Advance Processing . . .) is that this can significantly shorten your wait once you have access to your child. It is simply a matter of good planning and can save weeks of frustration at a later time while you wait for a document.

An I-600A, however, is good for only one year from the time they are accepted by the local INS office for processing. Then it will be necessary to resubmit everything including the $50 fee. The fingerprint charts are kept for 15 months to "cover" the period awaiting approval of the new set.

Your agency personnel should be completely familiar with the requirements pertaining to an international adoption. If they are not, or if you are pursuing a "parent-initiated" adoption, you can get a copy of the law—it is free and written in plain language. Single copies may be ordered from:

INS Outreach Program
424 I Street, N.W., Room 6230
Washington, D.C. 20536

Ask for M-249, "The Immigration of Adopted and Prospective Adopted Children."

U.S. GOVERNMENT INVOLVEMENT AND OTHER ORGANIZATIONS WHICH PARTICIPATE IN INTERNATIONAL ADOPTIONS

The individuals, official bureaucracies and placement agencies involved in international adoptions fall into four categories. Those categories, and the services provided, include:

(1) Federal Government Authority

As previously mentioned, the government of the United States allows parents to claim their foreign-born child as an "immediate relative." As a member of your family, the child is thus entitled to certain immigration privileges which would not otherwise be available to those born in a foreign country. The federal legislation that makes available this opportunity is **The Immigration and Nationality Act of 1952** (Title 8, U.S.C., Aliens and Nationality). Congressional authority for approving this claim and subsequently issuing a visa so the child can enter the United States rests with two different departments:

(a) The Immigration and Naturalization Service (INS) of the U.S. Department of Justice.

The Immigration and Naturalization Service has the responsibility of carrying out federal law concerning immigration and naturalization. Among other responsibilities the INS must process and approve the I-600 form, "Petition to Classify Orphan as an Immediate Relative." The process is accomplished in thirty-seven District Offices throughout the United States (see Appendix D).

(b) The Office of Visa Services of the United States Department of State.

This office is a division of the Bureau of Consular Affairs. It has officers located throughout the world, stationed in various U.S. Consulates. It is charged with the responsibility of investigating the circumstances of the orphaned child in that child's country of residence, and of approval and issuance of the child's visa.

(2) State Authority

The Constitution is a grant of authority by the states to the federal government. Powers not specifically granted the federal government are reserved to the states under the Tenth Amendment; **"The powers not delegated to the United States by the Constitution, nor prohibited by it to the states, are reserved to the states respectively, or to the people."** Since earliest times the states have held that measures to safeguard the health and welfare of their citizens lie within their authority. Fundamentally, adoption, as part of the public welfare is incorporated in the doctrine known as **"Police Power."** Simply put, police power is the authority of the people, vested in state government, to enact laws which protect the health and welfare of its citizens. It is concerned with the greatest good for the greatest number of people. With respect to adoption, the State Welfare Authority (known in many states as the Department of Social Services or Department of Human Resources) is charged with the responsibility of supervising adoption programs, including those for foreign-born children. The agency also has statutory responsibility for seeing that the provisions of the child welfare laws are carried out in accordance with the law. **This is why certain adoptions are perfectly acceptable in one state, but illegal in others.** You cannot rely on your experience or that of another person in another state to apply to your current state. If you assume the laws will be the same you may find yourself in a position of having spent much time and money for nothing; and having to repeat the process again!

(3) Child-Placing Resources (Agency)

One or more of five types of child-placing resources will be involved in an intercountry adoption.

(a) Domestic Adoption Agency — is licensed within its home state and provides adoptive services (which may or may not include child placement) for citizens of that state.

(b) Licensed Adoption Agent — is a licensed social worker who is authorized by the state (only in some states) to provide adoptive services such as doing a homestudy or provide post-placement supervision.

(c) Foreign Child-Placing Agency or Person — is permitted within the particular country to place children for adoption of facilitate an adoption. The placement may be either directly with an adoptive family, or with the assistance of a U.S.-based international child-placing agency.

(d) U.S.-Based International Child-Finding Organization (Liaison Organizations) — are incorporated, nonprofit groups who seek resources in foreign countries, advise families on how to proceed and work in conjunction with the family's homestudy agency. The organization may or may not be a licensed adoption agency. Since they are familiar with the intricacies of international adoption they can facilitate the paperwork and inform the local agency (such as Catholic Family Services, Lutheran Services, etc.) about the requirements for Immigration and the overseas courts. Examples would be **LIMIAR-USA,** and **Project Orphans Abroad.**

If the program is licensed (U.S.-based international child-placing agency) it can function as a liaison organization as well as an adoption agency by making placements directly with families and performing other adoptive functions such as the homestudy and post-placement supervision. If a licensed agency is working with a family in a state other than in the one in which it is licensed, the agency is functioning in the capacity of a liaison organization and not an adoption agency (which would require being licensed in that particular state).

(e) **U.S.-Based International Child-Placing Agency** — is a licensed agency which has a connection with a child-placing entity in another country. Such an agency may perform the duties of an agency with a particular family (conduct a homestudy and post-placement supervision) or function in the capacity of a liaison organization and refer a child to a domestic child-placing agency for placement of supervision. In some states, agencies can only conduct homestudies and provide supervision, but not actually take custody of a child. **Children's Hope is a U.S.-Based International Child-Placing Agency.**

(4) Parent-Groups

Parent-groups composed of individuals with a special interest in international adoption can be of the most valuable assistance to prospective parents. Such groups are usually aware of the most recent changes in adoption policy as well as which agencies are successful. These groups can be extremely helpful in enabling prospective parents to understand the complexities of adoption requirements and in assisting those parents to cut through red tape. They also function as a support group when prospective parents get discouraged because of the typical delays encountered in international adoption. Some agencies require clients to attend at least one parent group function during the homestudy process, since it is felt that an association with a parent group is in the best interest of the adopting family.

Parent-groups frequently publish newsletters which can be helpful to a family contemplating an intercountry adoption. Some newsletters can be localized to such a degree that they are not very useful; however, others may be very helpful and all are inexpensive if you wish to become a subscriber. The *OURS Magazine* started as a parent-group newsletter and has evolved into an important adoption resource of national significance. The subscription cost is $16 per year and this can be obtained from:

OURS Inc.
3307 Hwy 100 North, Suite 203
Minneapolis, Minnesota 55422

A list of OURS affiliated parent-groups may be obtained from OURS Inc. at the above address. If you are interested in subscribing to a particular newsletter you should write the parent-group and request a subscription. Through parent-group activities, you will come in contact with families who have completed international adoptions. Should you adopt a child from another country, these families will be part of a support group to help you and your child face the many problems and adjustments which may lie ahead. They will provide access to other children who share your child's background and physical characteristics — an invaluable aid in the healthy establishment of your child's identity.

TYPES OF ADOPTION

Agency Adoption

Agency Adoption is when the prospective parents pursue the child's adoption with the assistance of an agency. The agency involved will either be (1) a **U.S.-Based International Child-Placing Agency.** That is one, though located in the United States, which has a contractual agreement with an orphanage or individual in another country and thus has access to available children. The other type of agency with which prospective parents might work is a (2) **Domestic Child-Placing Agency** — one which works with an international child-placing agency in order to facilitate the desired adoption for a particular couple. An example of a domestic child-placing agency might be the State Welfare Department or private non-profit corporations such as Family Services, Catholic Family Services, or other organizations which have traditionally arranged adoptions of children within the United States.

When working with an agency, the prospective parents are assisted in the adoption process from start to finish by the agency personnel. The agency handles the paperwork for the parents and is instrumental in the selection and presentation of the child. The adoption is usually completed in the parents' state of residency and post-adoptive supervision usually occurs for a given period of time after the child is placed in the home.

Parent-Initiated (Direct) Adoption

When a couple makes contact with a foreign source and prepares the documents themselves, the process is referred to as direct, independent, or **parent-initiated adoption.** Yet, despite terminology, more and more agencies in recent years are assisting parents in this type of adoption. Basically, a parent-initiated adoption proceeds in one of the following ways:

WHEN THE ADOPTION IS DONE IN THE CHILD'S COUNTRY OF ORIGIN

With this type of adoption, the prospective parents work directly with an agency, orphanage, or individual in another country. The parents comply with all legal requirements of that country, including those for emigration, as well as U.S. immigration requirements. The adoption is finalized in the country of origin and the parents then return with their child to the United States. Occasionally, such an adoption can be done through a power of attorney, releasing the parents from the requirement to travel to the other country. However, in this circumstance, U.S. Immigration law requires that the child be **re-adopted** in the home state since the parents have not personally seen the child.

Parents may choose to readopt in their state of residence (if that is permissible), but it is usually not necessary to do so. The child will receive an IR-3 Visa status indicating it is not necessary to adopt in the United States for citizenship, as the adoption was properly completed abroad. In such a case the adoptive parents will need the assistance of an agency for the preparation of a homestudy. Depending on the country of the child's origin, other documentation may be required to be provided by a U.S. based agency working with the adoptive parents. Occasionally, the foreign source will request a letter of commitment from the U.S. based agency promising involvement for the required follow-up period. Honduras currently requests agency involvement with the adoptive family and progress reports on the child adopted for fourteen years following the adoption.

WHEN IT IS NOT NECESSARY FOR THE PARENTS TO GO TO THE COUNTRY OF ORIGIN

Again, the parents work with the foreign child-placing agency while at the same time completing **PREADOPTIVE REQUIREMENTS** in their state of residence. After their homestudy is complete and a child has been selected, a formal presentation is made by the foreign agency to the prospective parents. If the child is accepted and upon the completion of all emigration and immigration requirements, the child is brought to the United States to be adopted or readopted in the parents' state of residence. Because the parents will be adopting in the U.S., the child will be issued an IR-4 Visa classification. The parents must adopt the child in the U.S. before applying for the child's citizenship.

WHICH IS BEST, AGENCY ADOPTION OR PARENT-INITIATED ADOPTION?

This is a difficult question to answer and one which depends on each individual situation. There are advantages and disadvantages to either method. Let us first look at the more common approach, agency adoption, and secondly consider parent-initiated adoption.

CHOOSING A LICENSED AGENCY, ADOPTION FACILITATOR OR UNLICENSED AGENCY

There are numerous advantages to using an agency or liaison organization as opposed to trying to accomplish everything yourself. But **which** organization you use is of crucial importance. Not all states require a license for international child-placing agencies. If not licensed, an organization is not regulated by any outside body. Though they usually will be "non-profit, private corporations," that title does not address a code of ethics or standard of behavior. It is simply a legal designation that affords corporate protection against liability to the individuals involved in the enterprise as well as other business and tax advantages. Unlicensed agencies and liaison organizations do not provide homestudy, post-placement supervision or legal services. Examples of reputable programs in this category would be **International Mission of Hope,** and **Project Orphans Abroad.** These organizations have agreements with local, licensed agencies such as **Americans for International Aid and Adoption** and **Bethany Christians Services,** to do all the legal work, homestudy, and post-placement services. In this respect, these programs are bound by all the regulations of the licensed agency with which they are working. They may have the additional advantage of holding licenses in the foreign country from which they work.

The author believes that at the local level, it is extremely important to work with a licensed agency. These organizations will be regulated by administrative authority and must comply with standards set forth by the state legislature. A license is a fairly good indication that your child's adoption will be handled in an ethical and professional manner (of course, an indication is not a guarantee). The personnel in licensed agencies must be approved by the State Welfare Authority (The Department of Social Services, or Public Welfare). Each individual is judged on the basis of personal history (integrity), competency (education and training) and ability (experience), before the agency qualifies for a license. Such persons have usually been experienced in the process of adoption and have contacts in the various countries with which they have a working relationship. They know the adoption procedure and have the experience to handle unexpected problems that may arise. They also can specify what expenses you will incur during the process of adopting a child from a particular country.

At the local level, there are both licensed and unlicensed child-placing entities, including individuals who may or may not call themselves adoption-facilitators. These entities can find children overseas, but they cannot perform the legal work, do homestudies, or post-placement supervision. They do not have to play by the same rules as the licensed agencies and can make their own rules. They may make promises and establish practices which would be unthinkable for a licensed agency. If things don't go according to plan, prospective parents have little recourse when dealing with such people short of going to court. On the other hand, licensed agencies usually have a set of guidelines they are expected to adhere to in order to retain their license and reputation. For example, most agencies will have a policy, stipulated in writing, about how a client files a grievance if they are not satisfied with some aspect of the program. In addition, licensed agencies, being supervised by the state, usually must submit an annual financial audit and always are in jeopardy of losing their license if there is evidence of impropriety.

Obtaining a license to place children in adoptive homes is not an easy thing to accomplish. It requires a great deal of paperwork and organization. Aside from obtaining approval of personnel, the agency will be required to develop policies, plans, procedures, budget projections, etc., to meet state requirements. It can be a difficult and time-consuming process, which often seems far removed from the actual purpose for which the agency is being established. Some agency personnel may be too discouraged or impatient to attempt meeting license requirements.

The author does not mean to imply that the personnel in unlicensed agencies or, for that matter, private facilitators are not qualified or ethical. Such people may have the best intentions. But adoptions, especially international adoptions, usually contain more than enough frustration, delay and disappointment. A prospective parent should not therefore incur any additional risk in an already tenuous enterprise. Rather, they should do whatever they can to reduce their chances of something going wrong and try to ensure that their efforts will be rewarded. A state license is not a panacea. It is, however, one additional safeguard that the parents can acquire to ensure their success.

WHAT ABOUT DIRECT
OR PARENT-INITIATED ADOPTION?

There are advantages and disadvantages in choosing the path of parent-initiated adoption. If an individual has contacts in a foreign country, this method may be the better alternative. It would avoid the necessity of having to wait on a list for an indefinite period of time. It also affords the prospective parents the opportunity to be more directly involved with the adoption process and may even save the family some money. However, parent-initiated adoptions can be a tricky business, considerably more risky than using the services of experienced agency personnel. It can literally become a "tar baby" of delays, frustrations and unforeseen expenses. Consequently, it is an alternative that should be cautiously considered.

Even if a parent chooses this path to follow, he will still need to have minimal contact with an agency responsible for completion of a homestudy.

The following article on parent-initiated adoption was originally done by Richard Darby (1975), and revised by Phyllis Loewenstein (1978). It is reproduced by permission from International Adoptions, Inc., of Newton, Massachusetts.[4] I have included some of my own comments (in italics) to give emphasis or clarification.

"DIRECT OR
PARENT-INITIATED INTERCOUNTRY ADOPTIONS"
(From International Adoptions, Inc.)

Adopting a child from overseas without the use of an intercountry agency or organization can be an exciting and stimulating experience.

---

4. International Adoptions, Inc., 218 Walnut Street, Newton, Massachusetts 02160.

It requires a considerable amount of time, persistence, patience, and effort on your part. It is not a "short cut" to the adoption of an overseas child and should not be undertaken if you cannot commit extensive time and energy to the process.

There are many reasons why people decide to do a direct adoption. The adoptive parents that have assisted in direct adoptions have given us the following explanations:

(1) We want to give a home to a child who is not known to an intercountry adoption program and, therefore, might otherwise not be adopted.

(2) We want a child younger than those offered by the intercountry adoption programs.

(3) We wanted to adopt a child where no North American based adoption program is operating.

(4) We wanted to be totally involved in the adoption. By doing a direct adoption, we have more personal control over the progress.

(5) We enjoy doing things ourselves and are open to new ideas and cultural experiences.

(6) We intend to travel overseas and felt we could combine the adoption with our travel plans.

(7) If possible, we want to pick out the child ourselves.

There are some drawbacks to direct intercountry adoptions, and anyone intending to use this route to locate a child should be aware of and carefully weigh these considerations:

(1) Full Caucasian children are very difficult to obtain in this manner. In Europe adoptable children are in as great demand as in North America. Long waiting lists exist for the Caucasian child and most European countries do not allow the few young children available for adoption to be released for overseas placement. In Latin America most children available for adoption are Indian or Indian-Caucasian. Most sources in Latin America will NOT allow applicants to specify the skin tone of a child since this is subjective.

(2) In almost every case, applicants will be required to fly to the country of the child's birth and spend up to several weeks processing the adoption and making all necessary travel and visa arrangements. We recommend that you be prepared to fly to the country of the child's birth even if your source states that you do not have to do so. It could make the difference of adopting the child or not, should there be an unforeseen change in procedures.

(3) There is always the possibility that a source can "close" prior to your adoption. Laws, regulations, and procedures can change at any time without notice due to the political situation in the country of the child's birth.

(4) If something goes wrong in the adoption process, there is usually no agency to "back you up" or to take responsibility for the child. Since

the process is taking place overseas, the jurisdiction of U.S. courts or attorneys do not apply, and the American Embassy in the country of the child's birth is very limited in their ability to assist in adoption cases.

(5) Applicants to direct sources must be able to deal effectively and diplomatically with government bureaucrats and petty officials. Without a working knowledge of the language of the child's birth this can be difficult, although not impossible.

(6) Applicants must have sufficient time and assets to fly to the country of the child's birth for however long is necessary, pay doctor and lawyer fees, child care expenses, passport fees, as well as any unforeseen expenses.

(7) Applicants must be prepared to accept a child with undiagnosed or unforeseen medical problems, although a series of medical tests and a competent pediatrician overseas can minimize this possibility.

(8) Often there is very limited social information available on the child at the time of assignment, since most children are either orphaned or abandoned.

If you are willing to accept these limitations, then perhaps intercountry adoption is for you. Presently, most Latin American adoptions are direct adoptions.*

Before you begin your research, check with your local Immigration and Naturalization Service (INS) to be sure you are eligible. In most cases, one parent must be a U.S. citizen. However, non-U.S. citizens can adopt children by using a non-preference visa. If this is the case, be sure to find out from the INS which countries have short waiting lists for non-preference visas.

In general, any country that allows overseas adoptions will allow direct overseas adoptions. In the same respect, if you live in a state where independent U.S. adoptions are not allowed, make sure tht you will still be allowed to adopt directly from overseas. It is important that you deal with only LICENSED and/or LEGAL sources overseas. Some states that do not allow independent domestic adoptions will allow direct overseas adoptions as long as the sources you use are licensed or legal sources. This is also to your benefit in that it protects you from unknowingly adopting a "black market" child.

The first step in the direct adoption process is to find out what the pre-adoption requirements are for your state. You can check this information through your local INS office or State Department of Social Services. A home-study is required by a licensed adoption agency or social worker. Usually a licensed adoption agency can be found by looking in the Yellow Pages under "Adoption Agencies." Try to find an agency that is experienced in overseas adoptions.

---

*At the time of this writing, 1978, this statement was true. However, recently more and more Latin American countries are preferring to work with agencies and this is a trend which will probably continue.

If your state allows private social workers to do the home-study, be sure that the worker has had experience working with parents for overseas adoptions. Listings of social workers can also be found in the Yellow Pages or you can get a listing of social workers from your local adoptive parent group.

We cannot stress enough making contact with your local adoptive parent group. They generally prove to be an invaluable contact in every aspect of the adoption as a referral agency, support group, information source, etc. The local parent group often will have the latest information on procedures for direct adoptions from the country from which you wish to adopt.

Once you have the names of the social workers or agencies, request the following information from them:

(1) Will they do a home-study for a direct adoption through a legal source overseas? Mention that you will take full responsibility for locating the child and for processing the adoption.

(2) What is the length of time before the home-study can be started and how soon can it be completed?

(3) What fees are involved and for what services? Some agencies and social workers charge extra for post-placement services and legalization of the adoption. Others include it as part of the total fee.

(4) Will they accept responsibility for the placement once you and your child return to the U.S.?

When you have found the agency or worker to do your homestudy, the next step in your research is to begin to locate a source for a child. The first, and easiest, way is to speak to your local adoptive parent group. Most adoptive parent groups maintain up-to-date direct overseas sources which have proven to be reliable. If not, there are many excellent resources open to you.

If you are interested in locating your own source, you can take a number of different approaches. One way is to contact the embassy or consulate of the country from which you wish to adopt. The embassy is usually located in the capital city of the state. Ask them for information and procedures on adoptions of children from that country. Another approach is to write to the Welfare Department of the capital city in the country from which you wish to adopt. Several parents that we have assisted work for large multinational corporations and have obtained the names of reliable attorneys abroad who are willing to work with adoptive parents.

When writing overseas sources be sure to ask the following questions:

(1) Does the country allow a direct overseas adoption by a U.S. citizen?

(2) What are the laws, regulations, and procedures involved in adopting a child from that country? What are the restrictions?

(3) If writing the Welfare Department, ask if they have children available for adoption, what ages are currently available, and what are the procedures?

(4) If the Welfare Department does not have children available, would they send a list of licensed orphanages and child placing agencies that would be willing to work with U.S. families?

(5) Be sure to mention that you are having a home-study completed on your family, if this is the case.

Unless you have contacts in the country of the child's birth, it will most likely be necessary to go to that country and do all the processing yourself. If an overseas source is willing to work with you, you may be able to arrange to do some of this processing prior to your arrival. In any case, you will need to compile a dossier of documents on your family.

The overseas source will send you a complete list of the required documents. In most cases, these documents will have to be notarized, certified and authenticated. Most district courts or secretary of state's office can certify a notary's signature and authentication has to be done by the embassy or consulate of the country from which you wish to adopt.

Once the overseas source has located an appropriate child for you, they will usually send you a photograph and a socio-medical history on a particular child. When you receive this information, discuss it with your social worker to be sure this is the best possible placement for you. We also recommend that you discuss the medical information with a pediatrician familiar with overseas children. If you decide to adopt the child, notify the overseas source as quickly as possible.

Also during this time make an appointment with the appropriate INS official, who will explain the Immigration requirements for adopting independently from overseas. Each state has a slightly different procedure, depending on their interpretation of the laws.

Approval will then be given pending the receipt of the birth certificate and the release form on the child.

Let us assume that you are unable to find an orphanage or licensed child placing agency that will do any of the preliminary processing before you arrive in the country. If this is the case, make the arrangements with Immigration as outlined above (*usually, this requires filing the I-600A form and supporting documents*). When you fly to the country of the child's birth, locate the orphanage with which you corresponded and begin to make the arrangements with them for choosing the child and preparing to do the processing. You will have brought the I-600 form *and all the supporting documents* with you.

BE SURE THERE IS A BIRTH CERTIFICATE AND RELEASE FORM AVAILABLE ON THE CHILD. If the release is from an orphanage and it mentions the biological mother's name, you will need to obtain a decree from a governmental agency or the courts that a search for the biological mother was made and she could not be located. (This is usually handled by advertising the child in the local newspaper in the country of the child's birth). Otherwise, a release from the biological mother must also be obtained. We recommend that the release state that this is an unconditional surrender — an irrevocable release — and that the biological mother has signed the release without duress. This document should be notarized in the country of the child's birth. If the child has been declared orphaned or abandoned, court decrees will be necessary for documentation. This usually consists of a birth registration and a government release (usually granting adoption or guardianship to the adoptive parents).

Have the child checked out medically, and if possible, have diagnostic tests done. The medical report can be used as a guideline for the child's medical. The overseas source usually will have its own doctor, but take time to locate another pediatrician for a second opinion. If the child checks out medically, proceed to have legal work completed.

A word of caution, "healthy" is a relative term. Healthy children overseas are not healthy by U.S. standards. A healthy overseas child will, generally, be smaller than it's North American counterpart. The child may also have internal parasites, eye, ear, or skin infections, be undernourished and possibly have a slight upper-respiratory infection. These are all correctable problems that usually do not affect long-term development of the child. There is, however, always the possibility of an undiagnosed or unforeseen medical problem and parents must be prepared for this possibility. This is why we feel strongly that a second medical opinion is important.

The U.S. Consulate in the country of the child's birth can suggest reputable doctors and attorneys to process the child. Although most consulates will not make recommendations of one doctor or attorney over another, it is often possible to find out (usually from a secretary) who are the more reliable professionals. Once you have located an attorney, he/she would be able to handle legal work and obtain a passport for the child.

A word about fees: people in foreign countries often believe that Americans have unlimited sources of money. Before you contract with anybody to do work for you, whether an orphanage, attorney, or doctor, be sure that you agree in advance to fees involved. Otherwise you might find yourself paying for some "unforeseen" expenses. If possible, get fees in writing.

LINKED ADOPTION

Linked adoption is a term coined at Children's Hope. It is a "variation on a theme" of the traditional practice of parent-initiated adoption.

The difference is that the parent is not initiating the contact overseas; that is initiated by the agency. The agency makes the original contact and introduces the parents to the overseas child-finding source which may be an attorney, orphanage, or adoption facilitator. The agency also prepares the documents with the client's assistance and submits the proper documentation on behalf of the family. The agency agrees to do the required post-placement work and to regularly send the translated, post-placements reports, after the adoption is concluded.

Linked adoption is a combination of agency and parent-initiated adoption. The main difference between it and agency adoption is that the agency does not assume responsibility for the success or failure of that portion of the adoption process which occurs overseas. In this regard, it is more like a parent-initiated adoption because the parents must bear the risks themselves. The agency may require a family to sign a "statement of understanding," indicating the agency cannot be held accountable for those aspects of the adoption process for which it has no control. The statement might say that, at this point, the parents are working directly with the overseas contact and all adoption fees, foster-care payments, etc., are paid directly to those individuals. The agency will not resume a primary role in the adoption process until the parents return from overseas with their child.

Although at this point the parents are working directly with overseas contacts, that does not mean the agency has no role to play. They will still work with the families, providing orientation to the foreign country and the adoption process as it exists in that country. They will try and keep the family calm and informed as to what to expect next. The agency can also prepare the family's documents in a standard format which is acceptable to the foreign source and see that all the pre-adoptive requirements are met.

The crucial thing is that the family realize that at this phase of their adoption process the agency has little, if any, control and its role is clearly secondary. Consequently, the parents agree not to hold the agency responsible in the event something goes wrong overseas.

Though a linked-adoption may provide a legitimate adoption alternative for some people, it is clearly not for everyone. Those who pursue this avenue must be prepared to assume the same risks as those pursuing a parent-initiated adoption. They must be the type of individuals who can handle more stress than the average adopting family. Furthermore they must understand that there is **no absolute predictability** and there **are no guarantees;** yet, knowing this, they must still want to proceed.

CHAPTER FIVE

COMMENCING THE ADOPTION PROCESS

Preplacement Process and Agency Responsibility

SELECTING AN AGENCY

IF ONE BROWSES through the *Report on Foreign Adoption,* published annually by the International Concerns Committee for Children, he will see there are many organizations working in foreign countries to assist U.S. families wanting to adopt.* Working with one of these agencies means a contractual agreement and a commitment both on the part of the agency and the prospective parents. Adopting a child from a foreign country can be tedious and is frequently a confounding experience. You need to work with people in whom you have trust and confidence. You want an agency that will stand by you through the delays and setbacks and encourage your patience and optimism. Again, there is the very obvious matter of the considerable amount of time, money and hope you are investing in this organization; obviously you want to be selective.

When deciding with which agency to work, there are qualities you can look for to help you make as informed and intelligent a decision as possible. Some factors you should consider are:

(1) Is the agency licensed by the state in which it is located? A license itself is no guarantee, but it is an indication that the agency has adhered to the requirements set forth by the state licensing authority and that its operation is regularly reviewed by objective officials. The author cannot emphasize strongly enough: work with a licensed agency and/or a reputable liaison organization.

---

*The *Report on Foreign Adoption* is available from the International Concerns Committee for Children, 911 Cypress Drive, Boulder, CO 80303. A $15 donation is requested.

(2) From which countries is the agency finding the children? Adoptions proceed from Korea with far more regularity and predictability than they do from Latin America. Therefore if you are going to adopt from Latin America, don't expect it to go as smoothly (although in many instances it can) as a Korean adoption and don't compare it to your friend's adoption from Korea which went ever so nicely — it's not a valid comparison.

I remember receiving fund raising literature from Holt International Children's Services. Holt, of course, has done more Korean adoptions than anyone, yet when talking about adopting from Latin America, here is what they say in their literature.

> Dear Friend,
>
> "That's my Daddy"
> Every father loves to hear these words from his little son or daughter.
> These same words, however, have touched my heart with the urgency of homeless children in Latin America.
> Joe Hindman, Holt's representative in Latin America, recently came back from another trip, trying to move ahead Holt's programs in South and Central America. For Joe this trip brought some hope, but also a painful contact with the reality of waiting. Joe and his wife are trying to adopt a little girl in Bolivia.
> As a representative for Holt, Joe has the joy and pain of occasionally seeing Maria, the little girl he hopes to adopt. It's been a year since he began trying to adopt Maria. Joe still waits hopefully, but the uncertainty of Latin American adoption continues.
> "The last time I saw Maria," Joe said, "she and Cielo stood by my knees and watched me load my camera. Cielo is a little dwarf girl who also lives in the orphanage and is good friends with Maria. Maria does not talk much with me yet, and I sometimes wonder how she feels about me. When Maria stood by my knee, she looked at Cielo, saw her smiling up at me and said, 'Cielo, don't look at him like that. . . . He's **my** daddy!)"
> I'm sure Joe is tempted to just carry Maria away. But he can't. He looks in her eyes and sees the beginning of the bond between father and daughter, but he knows that adoption is currently on hold in that country.
> Then there is Cielo who can only look and hope. It might be a long time before she can say, "That's my Daddy."
> Adoption in Latin America is very difficult at present . . . almost impossible. But that doesn't mean that we should give up.
> I have no false hopes. Adoption is a volatile issue in many Latin American countries. In the last nine months I have seen four countries close down adoptions until they can rewrite the laws that govern adoption. The child welfare authorities have seen black market adoption, kidnapping — profiting by the lives of children. No wonder they move slowly and carefully and close down adoption entirely at the first rumor of scandal.

The problem for Holt and for the children is that the actions of a few unscrupulous people cause the doors to be closed on all, even those who serve children with integrity. That's why I ask for your prayers. . . . [1]

Whenever we have clients who try to compare adoptions from Latin America with those of Korea we give them a copy of this solicitation from Holt International Children's Service and ask them if they think the situations are the same!

(3) How long has the agency been in existence? What is their record of success? How many placements have they made in the last year? What are the experiences other persons have had in working with this agency? Will they release the names to you of clients who have successfully adopted through their program?

(4) Is the agency affiliated with state and national child welfare organizations? Such organizations provide support and continuing education for agency personnel so they can keep abreast of the ever-changing adoption scene. For example, Children's Hope is affiliated with the National Adoption Exchange, the Joint Council on International Childrens' Services From North America and the Michigan Association of Children's Alliances.

(5) Who are the persons involved in the agency? What are their reputations and motives? The Biblical wisdom, "a good name is better than precious ointments . . . " (Eccl. 7.1), applies here. Do you perceive a sense of commitment when working with these people or is it merely a job? Do they have adequate material describing their program? Are your calls and letters answered promptly and courteously? In short, do you feel these are people with whom you can work closely for a prolonged period of time? If possible you should try to obtain references on the personnel from clients who have previously worked with them. Another thing you can do is to **request a copy of their past licensing reports** from their state license consultant. This information is easily obtainable from the unit responsible for licensing adoption agencies within the State Department of Social Services. It will show you the agency's track record with regard to compliance with state licensing rules and will be a good indication of the agency's overall competency.

(6) Are there currently children available for adoption through this agency? If not, when will children be available? How long is their waiting list and where will you be placed on such a list? How many children

---

1. David H. Kim, *Prayer for Latin America* (Eugene, OR: Holt International Children's Services, 1987).

does the agency plan to place this year? The more ethical establishments will limit the numbers of those waiting to a reasonable number, so that people will not be waiting indefinitely. Don't be afraid to ask. If the answers are vague or elusive, beware!

However, you should remember that the agency can offer no guarantees—just estimates. Adoption programs can fluctuate greatly in any given country during the course of a year. It is often difficult to predict more than a few months in advance the status of a particular program. Your position on a list may vary depending on the age, sex and condition of the child you are willing to accept. For example, you may be the 10th person chronologically to enter a waiting pool of adoptive parents for Guatemala. However, if you are willing to accept a child of either sex, and a boy becomes available, that automatically puts you ahead of any family insisting they must have a girl. Also, if you are flexible with regard to age, this will advance your position. The same is true regarding medical conditions or handicaps. The broader you are in what you are willing to accept, the shorter will be your wait.

In any placement decision, the agency must consider the needs of the child, the length of time parents have been waiting, and the type of child parents are willing to receive into their family. For these reasons, it is usually not possible to give an exact answer as to your specific place in line. More likely you will be told "you are now in the top 5 families," or "next in line for the 1st healthy girl," or that "you have about 2 families in front of you." Your agency is not evading you—only trying to present a more realistic picture. In some programs the U.S. agency is not even referring the child; the decision is being made in the child's birth country by another organization and often with the birth mother's approval of a particular family. In such a situation it is impossible to pin-point any particular family's exact place in the waiting line.

(7) What are the financial responsibilities the adoptive parents must assume? Are the fees clearly delineated? Does the cost include a home-study, processing or administrative fee, overseas program fee, transportation? A reputable agency should be able to answer your questions about fees. Are any portion of the fees non-refundable if you decide to drop out or the program closes down?

(8) What must be completed in order to accomplish the adoption? What are the requirements? Is there follow-up after the adoption? Will a period of post-placement supervision be required?

(9) What are the specific requirements for international adoption in the parents' particular state? Does the state permit certain types of adoptions such as guardianships obtained overseas; does it allow you to readopt in your state if you choose?

After perusing the latest issue of the *Report on Foreign Adoption,* you might also contact your State Welfare Authority to see if any additional agencies are operating within your state. You will find that each agency has its own requirements and policies. In some cases, you will not be able to get on a list for a homestudy because there will be so many people waiting. You probably can facilitate matters somewhat if you know in advance what type of child you are looking for (age, sex, etc.) and can be specific in expressing your desires. Those agencies that can't help you should be in a position to indicate so immediately.

Finally, trust your instincts. If you feel put-off by agency personnel, if they seem cold and indifferent, these are probably not the people with whom you want to work. Your relationship with the agency you choose will be long and personal. You should be able to work with persons who can have empathy with your feelings, be supportive and optimistic.

The questions presented are just some of the things prospective parents want to ask themselves if they are to make an informed decision regarding the choice of an agency. Be aware, however, that as you are choosing an agency, **you in turn are being scrutinized by the agency personnel.** Many parents fail to realize this it is a two-way street!

Once you have chosen the agency you wish to work with, completed the formal application and remitted your application fee, you wait to see what will happen. **You have now begun the PREPLACEMENT process.** It doesn't matter whether or not you are planning a parent-initiated adoption or are going to use the services of an agency from start to finish. At this stage many of the requirements are identical and must be completed before any adoption is possible.

After submitting your application, you very likely will be contacted by the agency for an **assessment** and/or **orientation** interview. Some agencies have periodic group meetings of all prospective applicants to address questions the applicants might have. During an assessment session, the scope and services the agency provides will be explained. Agency personnel will inform you of the time required to complete a homestudy, when you can anticipate an offering for placement, and all of the legal requirements and the cost you can expect to incur. Of course, many of these questions have already been answered from telephone conversations with agency personnel or second hand sources (particularly parent groups or newsletters), but now the whole business is official.

At this point it is important to again emphasize that, in the same way you have been considering an agency, the agency personnel have been considering you as a potential client. Some applicants will not be accepted as clients from the start — too old, too many divorces, unrealistic expectations, etc. From **our experience** at Children's Hope, we have learned, that if there is anything that causes agency personnel not to want to begin a professional relationship with a client, it is what we perceive as a poor "attitude." When prospective parents exhibit an attitude that makes them unpleasant to work with, that is usually sufficient to preclude them from being accepted **by our agency** as clients. When they appear aggressive, demanding or abusive, the negative impact is significant. Believing that it is easier to prevent a problem than having to correct it later on, we just don't begin with such people. It should be emphasized, however, that this is the position of Children's Hope and we realize other agencies might feel entirely differently on this issue.

CHAPTER SIX

VIEWING THE CLIENT
THROUGH AGENCY EYES

PERCEPTIONS AND MISCONCEPTIONS

UNFORTUNATELY, many clients come to us with unrealistic expectations. Frequently we have the feeling some people believe adoption agencies are in the business of selling children. People come expecting the process to be rapid, without delay or problems and they often demand a guarantee as to the sex, age, precise skin color and state of health of the child. This attitude is evidenced by the frequently heard comment, "If I'm paying this money, shouldn't I be able to get exactly what I want?"

Sorry—no! **Adoption agencies are not in the business of selling children!** If the fees for adoption seem high, there is a reason—other than the profit motive (see an explanation of fees, Chapter 7). Legal expenses, translation costs, government authentications, orphanage contributions, maternity expenses for the birthmother, travel expenses for the prospective parents, etc.—all these add up and can be substantial. **YOU ARE PAYING FOR PROFESSIONAL SERVICES, NOT CHILDREN!**

THE REALITY OF INTERCOUNTRY ADOPTION

Intercountry adoption can be a frustratingly, difficult process. There can be disappointments and setbacks. Sometimes a placement is offered and a birthmother changes her mind. Such a situation, though devastating to the prospective parents, is completely legal and it is within the rights of the birthmother to do so. The International Concerns Committee for Children, recognizing all that can go wrong in an intercountry adoption, provides the following warning:

55

All of you need to understand that due to circumstances beyond the control of any agency, the possibility exists that the adoption process could be discontinued by foreign nationals, governmental action, or judicial decrees beyond the control of the agency. You must further understand that it is necessary to advance funds to accomplish agency objectives and a portion of those funds already utilized very possibly cannot be recovered in the event of such discontinuance. You need also understand that in spite of information to the contrary, the child, when received, might have some undiagnosed physical or mental problem or might develop such a problem at a later date. You need to know, finally, that despite agency effort to work with competent and honest lawyers, their actions are beyond agency control. This is by no means meant to scare you, but to tell you the simple facts of life about intercountry adoptions.[1]

Overseas, adoption is viewed differently than in the United States. It may be perceived as something shameful, an act which one does not wish to acknowledge in public. Ms. Nancy Cameron, the Director of LIMIAR U.S.A. has dealt very nicely with this subject in an article, "A View From the Other Side," published in the November/December 1986 issue of *OURS Magazine*. Ms. Cameron writes:

Month by month the value of this magazine is seen, heard, and felt in the lives of families already built by adoption and families seeking to adopt. Perhaps most readers rush quickly to those photographs of waiting children to ask the question, "Could this be the child we've so long awaited?" "Could we be the right parents for this particular child?" Then later readers scan the articles bearing testimonies of adoption experiences, sharing stories of the long wait, the difficulties, the problems, and the joys.

Today, I would like to add to these articles something less frequently told . . . the story on the other side of the world through the eyes of an organization which labors to help these very same children you await. Although I am speaking through personal experience in Brazil, surely my words could be repeated by organizations in many lands.

Although each adoption and each family and each situation is unique, by and large, the most common emotion first felt is joyful anticipation. Adoption of a foreign-born child into the North American family is generally perceived as something good, right, happy, and helpful to someone else as well as to the parent. Adoptive parents surround themselves with a network of support—a parent's group, an adoption agency, a social worker, even relatives—who also reflect and view the adoption as a positive experience. On the other hand, the foreign organization may be working in a totally hostile environment

1. *Report on Foreign Adoption* (Boulder, CO: International Concerns Committee for Children, 1987), p. 22.

where foreign adoption is legally possible but where the people see foreign adoption as a new concept, perhaps a disgrace as a recognition that the country cannot care for its own children.

Adoptive children within the foreign country may be regarded as second-class citizens — thus foreign adoptions may be perceived by the people as close to slavery or a vehicle for free labor. Adoption may become a popular topic in the news and press and sensationalized and distorted in order to capitalize on a mentality which would rather see children actually die in institutions or on streets than leave their native country. There, the topic of adoption may become a "political football" and used for discussions to elicit or damage careers and standings. In an area of intense hostility, the foreign workers often must put their reputation, careers, even lives on the line for your child — and on a daily basis. The work then becomes self-sacrificing beyond the imagination of the adopting parent.

Once adoptive parents begin the adoption process, they seek assurance that what they hope for will happen with a minimum of problems. That is certainly what the foreign organization desires also. However, predictability is difficult in an area where pioneer work is being accomplished; there is no precedent! In a large foreign country, the rules, laws, and procedures vary from state to state, province to province, city to city and even judge to judge. Often the procedures change within a single court from month to month. Then, too, with frequent changes of court workers or the entry of a new judge, the foreign worker must begin at square one to educate, sensitize, and convince about the rightness of foreign adoption. (As opposed to an independent lawyer, doctor, missionary, or a "contact," the foreign worker of a nonprofit, legal organization lays the groundwork for good program over and over, a lasting program . . . "a marathon and not a sprint.") Thus, accountability is most difficult, and adoptive parents must extend understanding to the difficulties the foreign workers confront daily.

Often heard complaints from American adoptive parents are the delays in the processing of the paperwork, the bureaucracy, the lack of comprehensive information, or misinformation. If there is one notable characteristic of us Americans as seen by other countries, then surely it must be our lack of patience. And patience, as so many of OURS Magazine articles emphatically state, is required.

One factor contributing to a delay in processing is that a court will seldom clarify the legal situation of one child out of the thousands it attends without cause. There is often a lack of record-keeping or sharing of information between court and orphanage. Often information is gathered only on a child at the time he enters the "system." (We have seen children suffer for years under wrong diagnoses, wrong labels, and consequently spend years in an inappropriate institutions). In a court handling thousands of cases, perhaps there is one typist, or one overburdened social worker unable to complete reports, make the visits and verify the facts for the judge. Courts and judges can and do intentionally lengthen and draw out their processing if their individual philosophies are not pro-foreign adoption.

American adoptive parents are called upon to make several financial expenditures in the course of the adoption. They usually do this cautiously knowing that the present and the past of foreign adoptions contain many abuses of money. It is a fact that any adoption program cannot operate on goodwill alone. The foreign organization initially can count on little or no financial support within its own country until the ideology of foreign adoption is embraced. And yet in the meantime there are mouths to feed and clothes, medicine, rent, hospitalization, dental treatment, school books, uniforms and tuition, salaries, travel expenses, accountant bills, telephone bills, Xerox bills, and telex bills to pay.

Adoptive parents must realize the importance their monies make and then they must ask questions: What is a reasonable fee charged by U.S. adoption agencies? How much of the fee goes to the foreign organization? What proof exists that the foreign organization receives its funds? Who or what in the foreign country receives those funds . . . the private lawyer or individual "facilitating" the adoption, or an organization financially supporting orphanages, individual families and children through sponsorship and projects to aid unadoptable children further? The grass roots funds raised by car washes, garage sales, church/school projects, and bake sales, are wonderful, and the enthusiasm the adoptive parents can bring to these events as a contribution to their child's care abroad should never be underestimated.

Think for a minute of the tremendous undertaking a foreign adoption is. Only until recently, with our modern and instant international communication systems has it been possible to dream that more than an occasional, isolated child could come to our country, to our very home, and become our child in a legal definition recognized by all the world's government. Indeed the idea is totally mind-boggling that foreign adoption is today possible within its existing scope.

Perhaps these words can broaden the understanding of the U.S. or Canadian family to the foreign organization. The foreign organization wants exactly what you want; it desires to see your child out of his strange world of institutionalization and into the warmth, love, and encouragement of your home. There is GREAT rejoicing when one child "comes home" but for the one child who has been so blessed, the foreign workers will remember children whom they could not extricate from the "system" or for whom death came before a family. They toil for your child under a taxing emotional, physical, and political burden. Extend to them your support, your prayers, your work, and your encouraging words.[2]

2. Nancy Cameron, "A View From the Other Side," *OURS: The Magazine of Adoptive Families,* Nov./Dec. 1986, p. 6.

Because of the potential problems and frustrations inherent in an international adoption, it becomes imperative that agencies select their clients carefully. Potential adoptive parents need to be individuals who can cope with the uncertainties and frustrations involved in a foreign adoption. Such people need to be mature, stable individuals who can deal with disappointment and remain patient and level-headed.

Individuals who appear unstable, over-anxious, or are demanding, aggressive, and in too much of a hurry — as well as those who react to frustration in an hysterical manner, or change their minds every few days might find themselves rejected from the list of prospective applicants. Such persons appear to be poor choices for international adoption.

How selective a program will be in choosing its clients will depend upon many things, most importantly the agency's **motive for existing.** If profit is their primary motivation, then their standards will likely be lower, basically being whether or not the client can afford and is willing to pay the agency fees. It is a fact, however, that many programs (such as Children's Hope) have been started by adoptive parents who, having achieved their initial goal, were interested in helping others to adopt. Such individuals are motivated more by a sense of commitment than by financial reward.

If a program is motivated primarily for money, this fact will soon emerge. They will usually treat adoptive parents poorly and show little interest in the welfare of the children. The only way to know this is to inquire from others as to past experience. Again, you can check with parent groups, request state licensing reports, and contact the Better Business Bureau in their community as well as the International Concerns Committee for Children in Boulder, Colorado.

REQUIREMENTS FOR PROSPECTIVE PARENTS

The requirements for adoption through whichever program selected will vary considerably. Some programs will have rigid criteria (the Korean government establishes their criteria) on such aspects as number of children already in the family, age of parents, length of marriage, number of previous divorces or religious affiliation. If a program is networked to another program, it will likely have the same criteria as the larger program. The criteria of the Los Ninos Adoption Center are quite liberal and when Children's Hope was associated with that organization as a networking agency we simply adopted their criteria with little alteration. As stated in the handbook of the Los Ninos International Adoption Center:

"Adoptive parents must be racially tolerant, flexible about adoption arrangements, patient concerning the wait for a legally adoptable child, and willing to accept a child of either sex. We will consider your preference when we make an assignment. (We) accept single persons and couples married one year, between the ages of 25 and 55, with or without children, of all races and religious affiliations, with sufficient income to pay the adoption expenses and raise a child. Previous divorce is acceptable. Applicants with chronic diseases and handicaps are also considered."[3]

Religious Requirements

Since many adoption programs have been started or are supported by a particular church it is not uncommon to find clients restricted to that particular denomination. This should be one of the first questions asked by prospective parents when investigating a potential program.

Children's Hope, like many international adoption programs is nonsectarian with respect to religion. However, we believe religious training can play an important role in a child's well being. For this reason, Children's Hope looks favorably on parents who have a commitment with a church or synagogue.

Choosing to Represent a Client — Agency Prerogative

Does an agency have the right not to accept a client, for "whatever" reason? This, to the best of the writer's knowledge, has not been tested in court. However, at Children's Hope, we have always been selective in whom we will accept. Even though our general requirements are liberal **we screen applications carefully.** We continue to maintain that we have the right to exclude applicants. Until this is contradicted by a judicial decision, we will continue to believe **our primary responsibility is as advocate of the child** and will scrutinize our applicants carefully.

As stated in the *Children's Hope Handbook:*

"Children's Hope reserves the right to not work with any family or individual. Categorically, and because of criteria established by the

---

3. *Los Ninos International Handbook,* (Austin, Texas: Los Ninos International Adoption Center, 1986), p. 1.

Immigration and Naturalization Service (INS), we will reject automatically, person who have been convicted of felony crimes, or mentally ill persons or those with a recurring (continuing) problem of drug and/or alcohol abuse.

Individuals who have a Protective Services complaint against them and are so listed in the Department of Social Services computer files will also be excluded. Such individuals need to have their file expunged before Children's Hope can consider placing a child in that family. We realize, however, that each situation is distinct. Individual circumstances are taken into consideration and decisions made only after extensive investigation and evaluation."[4]

It would seem from the foregoing that we select clients capriciously. Nothing could be further from the truth. In fact, all clients are carefully evaluated during a two-hour required assessment interview and most are required to undergo a complete battery of psychological tests. We elected not to accept clients for many reasons, including:

- One parent wanted to adopt, but the other didn't.
- The family couldn't afford the expense of an adoption.
- The family had significant problems raising other children.
- The applicant had a protective service complaint filed against him/her or prior criminal convictions.
- The applicant practiced child-rearing practices which we felt inappropriate, bizarre, or harmful to a child's physical or mental well being.

Less specific, but just as important is the attitude the prospective parents exhibit during the interview or afterward in the initial stages of the adoption procedure.

We have terminated our professional relationship with prospective parents, after beginning, in only a few cases. However, as mentioned before, we reserve the right not to work with people whom we feel are or will become problematic. Since international adoption is a difficult and long road to follow, it is only natural that we want to make it with traveling companions with whom we are comfortable. When prospective parents develop an attitude that makes them unpleasant to work with, that is usually sufficient to warrant terminating the relationship.

Things we find especially disagreeable are when parents become aggressive, when they make repeated phone calls to the agency and demand to know why things are not moving more rapidly, or as to what precise date they will get their child or what is their number on the list. If

---

4. James Pahz and Cheryl Pahz, *Children's Hope Handbook: Policies and Procedures,* 4th ed. (Shepherd, MI: Children's Hope Adoption Services, 1987), pp. 15-16.

they remark or imply that the agency does not have the parent's interest at heart or that the agency is dishonest and only interested in making money, that is usually sufficient to end our accord.

Although in almost every case we have terminated our professional relationship before the homestudy was undertaken, we have on one occasion refused to continue working with a family, after a homestudy had been approved. Even with the realization that it was our job to help families deal with the stresses of foreign adoption, this family had become so aggressive and bothersome that we felt justified in discontinuing our professional activities on their behalf.

SOME QUESTIONS FREQUENTLY ASKED BY PROSPECTIVE PARENTS

(1) Why must fees be so high? Why is it necessary for a non-profit corporation to charge any more than the actual dollar figure needed for an adoption?

Fees are determined upon two factors: (1) the overseas expenses — lawyer's fees, medical fees, foster care expenses, orphanage contributions, etc. and (2) agency expenses — overhead, administration and salaries. As in any business, there are certain necessary expenses, i.e., rent, electricity, telephone (telephone bills are enormous), printing and photocopying, postage, as well as compensation for workers.

It is also necessary that funds be set aside for unfortunate emergencies. For example, on one occasion a birthmother relinquished her baby to us in Guatemala. We kept the baby in foster care for four months paying a foster care payment of $150 each month. During the final hearing, and after the child had been assigned a family, the birthmother began to weep and told the Judge she had changed her mind. The child was returned to the birthmother and Children's Hope was presented with a $500 legal bill. That bill, as well as the foster care payments, were paid by the agency and not the prospective adoptive parents. It represented a financial loss of over a thousand dollars.

Although such occurrences are not regular, they do occasionally happen and an agency must be financially prepared for such a contingency if it is to remain financially viable. The best way to prepare for such an event is to charge each family a little more money so there will be funds for a rainy day. That way, like group insurance, each adoptive family is contributing a small percentage to help if one particular adoption incurs unexpected expenses.

(2) Why is it necessary to pay full payment in advance of service?

At Children's Hope, we have learned to our disappointment to be somewhat distrustful of people. When we started our agency we had flexible payment arrangements for anyone who made such a request. We didn't ask for fees until after the service was rendered. For example, we didn't require parents to pay a post-placement supervision fee until after a child was placed in the home. We soon learned that although we had to make post-placement supervision visits as required by Michigan law, some families refused to pay for this service, deciding they had already paid enough money for their adoption. Thus, the service had to be done at the expense of the adoption agency. The money, of course, had to come from somewhere which really meant that other clients were in fact subsidizing portions of the adoption expenses for families who refused to pay.

In other cases we accepted partial payment plans from people believing they would pay as promised, only to be told later they couldn't afford it. After two years of operation, we finally decided that each family must pay their full adoption expense in advance. If they were unable to do this, we assumed they were not financially capable of supporting the child and we refused to accept them as clients.

(3) Why are some families refused the services of an agency?

Again, all we have to use for an example, is our own program, Children's Hope. At our agency, our foremost concern is the child's welfare. If we feel a child would not benefit by being placed with a particular family, we will not approve a family's homestudy. **We regard ourselves as advocates of the child first and only secondly to the parents.** In other words, we represent the child although the parents pay the bill!

(4) Why can't you specify the sex of the child? Are there times when you can specify the sex?

Most overseas programs insist that prospective parents be willing to accept a child of **either sex.** Parents may state their preference for a boy or girl and should give their reasons for that preference. If their reason is good (i.e. they already have two children of the same sex) most agencies will try to do whatever is possible to help them get their wish. However, there is no guarantee that a preference will be honored unless specifically so stated.

At Children's Hope, like many adoption programs, about three out of four adoptive families indicate a preference for a girl. This phenomena has been observed by others and apparently has to do with the belief that "foreign-born females are easier to parent with fewer risks and difficulties, both medically and behaviorally."[5]

Unfortunately for these parents, three out of four children placed for adoption in Latin America are boys! It is a difficult problem and the simplest remedy is to require parents to be willing to accept either sex.

(5) If I reject a placement will I go to the bottom of the waiting list?

No, especially if you have a good reason for rejecting the referral.

However, most agencies have many families waiting and try to present the placement offerings in as fair a manner as possible — going around to as many families as possible. If a family refuses more than two appropriate referrals they should expect a longer period of time to elapse before a new offering will be rendered. Exactly how long will depend upon the number of other families waiting.

(6) When does the clock start running?

At Children's Hope, the clock starts running with respect to receiving a referral from the time the client's **formal adoption dossier** is submitted to the program or attorney overseas. Some clients are very slow in getting the required documents to us but others will have them ready quickly. These documents must be certified, authenticated and forwarded overseas. We tell our clients that from the time the documents are sent, it should take approximately (X) months — depending on the program and country.

(7) If I get pregnant while waiting for a referral, will that nullify my application?

It might. Although we recognize that if such an event occurs the parents could be twice blessed, we still need to remember that our primary concern is with the adopted child. Consequently, although we are happy for the parents, we must put the child's interests ahead of the parents. The decision of whether or not to continue with the adoption must be made by the prospective parents and the social service worker together. Each case will need to be judged on an individual basis. Some foreign countries require a signed statement that you will not add to your family by birth or adoption for at least one year following placement. Whether or not such a provision is legally enforceable, however, is highly questionable.

---

5. W. Robert Lange, MD, MPH and Ellen Warnock-Eckhart, MSW, "Selected Infectious Disease Risks in International Adoptees," *The Pediatric Infectious Disease Journal,* 6, No. 5, (1987), 447-450.

WHAT AGENCIES EXPECT FROM CLIENTS

Honesty — a homestudy is only useful if it is done in good faith, with candor and honesty. Since clients are being evaluated it is natural to want to put one's "best foot forward." However, sometimes, in an effort to do so, clients omit or distort important events which they feel might have a negative bearing on their evaluation. Experience has shown it is better to be open with your worker in advance than to have negative information come out later. This is especially true of past behaviors (mistakes) which you might feel have now changed. Should negative information surface from a routine police or protective service investigation, it will be difficult for the agency to remain impartial. You must believe that the worker is there to help you and will do his or her best on your behalf.

Cooperation — The agency cannot do it all. In the scheduling of appointments, gathering documents, etc. your caseworker depends upon your assistance. Most of your documents must be gathered before your homestudy can be reviewed. The responsibility to get these required documents to your agency in a timely manner rests with you, the client.

Common Sense — Agency personnel are usually very busy. Although most want to answer your questions and be accessible to families, clients should not call **too often** for "progress reports." Talk with your worker and set up a schedule so that you can receive feedback about the progress of your adoption. For example, "If I haven't heard anything in 3 months, I'll give you a call," or, "Since you told me I would hear about the paperwork in 6 weeks, may I call if no news has arrived by that time"? By making such arrangements in advance, you receive the information you need (if your file is lost or forgotten, you can remind them), yet you will be not perceived of as a nuisance by the agency staff.

Be Patient — Believe that your agency has your interest at heart and is doing all possible to facilitate your child's adoption. Don't call weekly to ask when your baby is coming. When the agency knows, you can rest assured, you will be the first they tell. Try and keep informed by reading agency mailings and newsletters, by participating in your local parent group, and through the schedule of contacts you have set with your social worker. Of course, this is easier said than done!

CHAPTER SEVEN

DOCUMENTATION

I F THE AGENCY believes you to be a good candidate they will provide additional material to be filled out requesting information about your family, background, financial status and parenting abilities. This information will be used to provide preliminary data to your social service worker in preparing for your homestudy.

Federal regulations require that the homestudy must contain, but is not necessarily limited to the following:

1. The financial ability of the adoptive or prospective parent or parents to rear and educate the child.
2. A detailed description of the living accommodations where the adoptive or prospective parent or parents currently reside.
3. A detailed description of the living accommodations where the child will reside.
4. A factual evaluation of the physical, mental, and moral ability of the adoptive or prospective parent or parents to rear and educate the child.[1]

This information will also be required by the State Welfare Authority and, in almost every case, the foreign government of the country in which you will be adopting.

In addition to the homestudy document, you will be required to present other documents. These items are necessary for Immigration processing, for foreign courts, probate court, and to verify facts in the homestudy. You will need to prepare your documents in special ways to satisfy the various officials to whom they are to be presented. For some documents you will need only one official copy; others you will need to get in duplicate or triplicate.

---

1. *The Immigration of Adopted and Prospective Adoptive Children,* Dept. of Justice, Immigration and Naturalization Service Form M-249 (Washington, D.C.: Government Printing Office, 1984), p. 9.

Following, you will find a description of the documents necessary for your dossier and Immigration requirements. After each document is an explanation of how the document should be prepared and the number of original or official copies you will need. This is a general guideline for most Latin American countries; however, variations may occur within different programs. Should the country or program of your choice require different or additional documentation, you would be notified and guided in this regard.

HOW DOCUMENTS SHOULD BE PREPARED

Before listing the documents, we wish to briefly describe the methods of preparing your documents so they will be acceptable for foreign adoption purposes. Documents which are improperly prepared will not be acceptable to officials from the Immigration and Naturalization Services. Such documents will need to be redone, creating additional time and work for yourself and the agency staff.

1. Some documents (such as those presented to Immigration to verify your financial status) do not need any special preparation — however, **THEY MUST BEAR THE ORIGINAL SIGNATURE OF THE INDIVIDUAL PREPARING THE DOCUMENT.** A photocopied signature is not acceptable.

2. Documents such as birth certificates, marriage certificates, and divorce decrees will need to be **certified copies.** Certified copies can be obtained from the county in which the birth, marriage, or divorce occurred, or from the Bureau of Vital Statistics in the state where they occurred.

   To order a certified copy it is advised that you telephone in advance to find out the fees for this service. In many cases, if you have a credit card, you may charge the fees directly to your account and the documents can be sent to you immediately. Otherwise it may take a few weeks to receive your certified copies.

3. To be acceptable to foreign courts, your documents will need to go through a process of notarization, verification, and authentication. Certified documents need only be authenticated, although some countries may require all certified documents to have a seal from the Secretary of State office. It is not difficult to prepare your documents properly, so long as specific instructions are followed.

(A) Notarization — this means that the document is signed in front of a notary public **who verifies that the signature is valid.** The notary will sign the document and then must type, stamp, or print his/her name, county and state of registration as a notary, and state that his/her commission expires on a particular date. It is best to have the notary place an official seal on the document.

(B) Verification — means that the Notary (who witnessed your signature) is duly registered with the Office of the Secretary of State in a particular state. Once the document has been notarized, it can be verified in either of two different ways:

    (1) You can take the document to the County Clerk of the county in which the notary is registered and request a **"certification of the notary."** The fee for this varies for each county, usually being twenty-five cents to $1 per document.

    (2) All the documents to be verified can be sent to the **Secretary of State,** since all notaries are registered with the Secretary of State. The fee for this service can vary from state to state, so it is important to check the fee in advance and enclose the proper payment when requesting this from your Secretary of State. It is also best to include a note describing the purpose and country for which the documents are intended to be used. Also, enclose a stamped, self-addressed envelope for the return of the documents to you. It is suggested you send this material by certified mail.

(C) Authentication — documents which have been properly notarized and verified are ready for the final step of processing, authentication. These documents are sent to the Consulate of the country from which you intend to adopt. **The "authenticity" of your documents is verified by the signature and seal of the Consul General.** The cost for this service varies with the country. The Chilean consulate in Chicago does not charge an authentication fee for documents which are to be used in an adoption. The consulates of other countries charge fees ranging from $5 to $25 per document. It is a good idea to call the consulate ahead and inquire what the charge will be.

REQUIRED DOCUMENTS

At Children's Hope we request parents to forward required documents to our agency since we assist clients with Immigration and formal dossier preparation. However, many agencies leave these details to the client. **It is very important that you check with your agency to see if they handle the "pre-filing" for you or if they expect you to do this yourself.** Exactly which documents you submit to your agency or who prepares and forwards the final papers will be explained by your agency representative.

If you provide photocopies along with the original and certified documents you submit to the Immigration and Naturalization Service, they will keep the photocopies and return the originals for some documents. It is a good idea to keep any of your returned original papers together, so should something go wrong, you will at least have some original documents.

Certified Birth Certificates — order three for each adoptive parent. You keep one for obtaining your passport, the other two are for your immigration clearance and your foreign dossier.

Certified Divorce Decrees — order two for each divorce. One is for the foreign courts and one is for Immigration.

Certified Death Certificate — order two if you were previously married to a spouse who died. One is for the Immigration and Naturalization Service, one is for your dossier.

Certified Marriage License — order two. One is for the Immigration and Naturalization Service and one is for your adoption dossier.

Medical Examination Form — one notarized and verified form for each adoptive parent. **Medicals for ALL members living in a household must usually be presented for homestudy approval.** Only the adoptive parents' medicals need to be notarized and verified for the foreign dossier.

If you are an infertile couple or have been undergoing infertility testing, it may be helpful to obtain a letter from your physician or specialist stating this. This can be an advantage in some programs that give preference to such persons. Such a letter should be on a letterhead, signed by the physician, and sent directly to the adoption agency.

Police Clearance — one for each adoptive parent. You usually need only complete an agency form, sign and return it to your caseworker. Your agency will instruct you.

Department of Social Service Clearance (Protective Services Division) — one for each adoptive parent if required in your state. Your Social Service Worker will present you with the form. You complete and sign the appropriate section and return it to your caseworker. This form **does not need to be notarized or verified.**

Reference Letters — you will need original letters of reference from three separate references. In order to be used overseas, your references will need to have their signatures notarized and the letter will also need a verification of the notary so that it can be authenticated.

Choosing the people to be your references is very important. They should be individuals who are both capable and willing to take the time to write a letter on your behalf and go to the trouble of having their signature notarized. Ideally they should have seen you with children or have been in your home so that they can write first hand about all your good qualities. If such individuals are "professionals" who can write their letters on letterhead stationary, this may be advantageous, although not absolutely necessary. Likewise, a letter from a priest or minister is also desirable, but not usually necessary. The important thing is that the letters be neat, well written, and discuss the issues relevant to your child-rearing potential.

At Children's Hope, a form is sent to references after the Social Service Worker has contacted them by telephone. The reference letter form lists instructions and guidelines to be followed in preparing the requested reference letter. Although well-intentioned, some references are not always quick to respond to this request and delay writing their letters. It is probably a good idea for the adoptive parent to periodically check to see which letters have arrived and which individuals need a friendly reminder.

Employment Letters — two original letters for each employed applicant. One need only be signed; the other must be signed, notarized, and verified. The letter should state your job title, length of employment, your annual salary and benefits, and statement as to whether your position is permanent or temporary.

Statement of Net Worth — you will need two of these. One needs only be signed by the applicants; the other needs to be signed, notarized, and verified.

Letter From Your Financial Institution — you will need two of these. One needs to be only a signed original; the other must be signed, notarized, and verified. The letter should indicate the date the account was opened, the total amount deposited for the past year, and the present balance. A separate letter will be needed for each account (checking, savings, etc.).

Copy of Your Last Income Tax Return Filed (1040 Form) — you will need two of these made from your client copy of the form. For one, the photocopy is acceptable as is; the other will need to be notarized by signing it in front of a notary public and then having the document verified.

Letter Stating Your Desire to Adopt — you will need one, notarized and verified. Each applicant (or couple) is requested to write a letter describing themselves, their community, and their interest in adoption. A sample letter is included in Appendix A for your information, but this is only offered as a guide as to some of the information you might wish to include. For most programs a one-page letter should be adequate.

Adoptive Homestudy — Your homestudy document should be properly prepared for Immigration and the foreign courts, as well as your state probate court (should you need to adopt in your state of residence). Your agency will be responsible for providing this. One notarized, verified, and authenticated copy will be needed for overseas.

Letter of Commitment by Supervising Agency — Your agency will provide an authenticated letter stating their commitment to the foreign government to provide adoptive assistance and to supervise for a period of time after the child is placed with your family. The letter will indicate the agency's willingness to provide periodic documentation to the foreign court indicating the progress your child is making for a specified period of time. This is required only in some programs and countries, not all.

Photographs — Applicants are usually requested to submit photographs of themselves and their home (inside and outside). The actual number and type of photographs differ with various programs, and during the homestudy process your caseworker should be advising you in this matter.

Power of Attorney — one or two official copies, signed, notarized and verified. At some point in your adoption process it may be necessary for you to have a properly prepared Power of Attorney form so that an attorney in the foreign country of your choice will be able to represent you in your adoption proceedings. This form varies, depending upon the country and the attorney (for some countries, you may need to sign two powers — one for the attorney, and one for the representative who does all the "running-around" with your documents).

Passports — each adoptive parent should obtain a valid passport, even if only one plans to travel. This is because foreign courts often require passport numbers as a means of identification. Also, your adoption plans may change, or unforeseen events occur which would affect travel plans. In addition, foreign requirements can change without notice, making travel by both parents necessary in a program which previously required only one parent to travel. You should apply for your passports during the homestudy process. About three to four weeks after your application you should receive your passport and which is good for ten years.

Passport applications can be obtained from your local post office or Office of the County Clerk. Along with the completed form and fee, you will need to submit two 2" × 2" color photos (passport photos) and a certified copy of your birth certificate. Your local Automobile Association of America (AAA) is a good place to inquire about having passport photos taken.

Psychological Report — some countries (or specific programs) require a psychological report as part of their documentation. If that is the case, your agency should advise you. At Children's Hope, we reserve the right to require a psychological evaluation on any family for whom concern arises during the homestudy or homestudy review process.

Household Water Requirements — in some cases, if a household does not have city water they may be required to have a water safety-check by the public health authority. This is not a water analysis, but only a check that the water is potable. This service is usually free, but some counties charge a small fee.

Immigration — I-600A Application for Advance Processing — in the immigration packet you will find: 4 fingerprint cards (two per adoptive applicant), an I-600A form (orange), an I-600 form (blue), and an Affidavit of Support form (white). Put the white and blue forms in a safe place for later use after your child has been located. Initially you will need only the fingerprint charts and the orange form.

> **Step 1** — each applicant fills out the requested information on the fingerprint charts. There will be two charts per person. Read the top portion of the charts and fill in as completely as possible. Don't forget to sign the charts.
>
> **Step 2** — have your fingerprints taken at the local police or sheriff's office. Call in advance to explain what you need, and find out the best time to have your fingerprints taken. There is usually no charge for this service.
>
> **Step 3** — fill out the front and back page of the orange form. Each applicant must sign and date the appropriate boxes below block II. The person who fills out the form is the prospective petitioner and must be a U.S. citizen.

Step 4—send the fingerprint charts, the completed orange form, and a check made out to the Immigration and Naturalization Service for $50 directly to the INS office or to your adoption agency. At Children's Hope we ask our clients to send this to our office where we make photocopies of the documents for the client's file, as well as check the accuracy of your forms. We also note the date your application was submitted to Immigration. Next we forward your material and the necessary supporting documents to Immigration. Once all your Immigration material is submitted, we keep track of your status until Immigration issues a determination in your case.

If you are handling your Immigration Pre-Clearance instead of your agency, then you will also need to submit to the Immigration and Naturalization Services all the following supporting documents applicable to your situation.

(1) Certified birth certificate for each applicant.
(2) Certified marriage certificate.
(3) Certified divorce decrees.
(4) Certified death certificate of former spouse.
(5) Approved homestudy with statement indicating the time period for which the agency's license is valid.
(6) Employment verification letter with original signature.
(7) Statement of net worth.
(8) Most recent copy of your income tax (1040) form.
(9) Letter from financial institution with original signature.

REMEMBER: Your agency is there to advise and assist you in your adoption procedures. Acquiring proper documentation can be frustrating and confusing. During the homestudy process your worker should answer your questions and be able to explain routine adoption procedures to you. You should feel free to contact your agency if you have questions; that is one of the reasons most adopting families decide to use an agency.

THE HOMESTUDY PROCESS

The written evaluation on an applicant's capacity for parenthood is known as a HOMESTUDY. It is through the process of conducting the homestudy that the agency determines whether or not a particular individual or set of parents can provide a suitable home environment for a child. It is also a time that affords mutual exploration into feelings and attitudes the parents may possess concerning adoption and, in particular, adopting a foreign-born child. In addition, it can serve as an initial preparation for the challenge and concerns of being an adoptive parent.

Many prospective parents abhor the idea of a social worker coming into their home and "snooping around" — passing judgement and generally making their lives miserable! On the occasions the worker is due to arrive the parent cleans diligently, dresses in his/her best and tries to anticipate the questions that will be asked as well as the answers for which the social service worker is looking.

Probably, in the whole adoption process, there is nothing more misunderstood than the purpose of the homestudy! Children's Hope tries to make it clear to the prospective parents that the homestudy is a process during which the social service worker can gather facts that will be needed by the courts, government agencies and foreign government. At the same time, it is a way that parents can explore with a trained professional their expectations and the realities of adoption. They can receive the answers they may have concerning questions about the children the agency has available, the culture from which the child comes, or special needs such children have.

It is understandable that the parents should be anxious and want to put their best foot forward. But whether or not the house is spotless or the clothes fashionable is unimportant. The social service worker is not interested in the superficial aspects of appearance, but in the substance of the marriage (if it is a couple) and the quality of the home environment.

Children's Hope usually requires four visits to complete a homestudy — two at the applicant's home and two in the agency office. Other agencies might specify a different number of visits. For instance, some agencies have group meetings of several families in the homestudy process with individual interviews on separate days. The length of time spent for each visit is approximately two hours and the couple will be interviewed together as well as individually. The entire process takes between one and three months to complete. We try to make the actual visits informal and comfortable, usually with coffee or other refreshment. The social service worker asks questions concerning the marriage (if a couple), relationships with children and other family members, reasons for wanting to adopt and so forth. The worker may read the questions from a prepared form or merely be extemporaneous. He/she will also want to see your other children, if you have children.

The relationship between the prospective parent(s) and the social service worker during the homestudy process should be positive. The parents should feel the caseworker is a caring, empathic individual who is on their side. The worker should behave in a professional manner and ask questions that are germane to adoption.

What can you do if you are uncomfortable with your worker?

If you feel the episode is not going the way you would like, or if you perceive that the worker is uncaring or insensitive, if he/she is asking questions you believe to be too personal or not pertinent to the subject, you should speak up. Express your feelings to the worker. He/she might be baiting you to elicit a response. If not, it is still better to be honest and confront the issue. If this doesn't help, contact the worker's supervisor and request a meeting with the worker and supervisor. Explain your concerns and indicate your feelings that you feel you could work better with another worker. This may be difficult to do, but in the long run you may be better served. After all, you have paid a fee for a professional service (the homestudy) and you have a right to have a worker in which you have confidence.

Your social service worker should keep you informed of the progress of the homestudy and when you can expect it to be finished. If there are concerns, they will be shared with you during the study. Agency procedures for homestudy review differ. At Children's Hope, we send a letter to the clients shortly before the completion of the study indicating it is about to be formally reviewed at the next scheduled Homestudy Review Meeting.

Upon completion of the homestudy, the social service worker writes a final report and makes his/her **recommendation** to the supervisor. The study is then reviewed (at Children's Hope) at the specially designated meeting. The Homestudy Review Committee (composed of all workers and the social service supervisor) reviews all studies and renders a determination as to whether or not to approve the family for adoptive placement. At Children's Hope, this is a group decision. The decision may be an "unconditional approval" or, if the committee feels more information is needed, it may postpone a decision contingent upon additional testing and/or other information. It may put a "hold" on the adoption process if it feels the family still has issues to resolve.

A "conditional" approval might require that the parents seek counseling or complete a course in "effective parenting" or some other subject the committee feels is appropriate before the final approval can be rendered. Then too, the committee may decide to "disapprove" a family if it feels it is in the best interest of a child to do so. A "disapproval" means that, in the committee's view, it would not be wise to place a child with this particular family.

The report will become part of the official record. Traditionally, the document was seldom shared with the prospective parents. In some states, a copy of the homestudy **must be provided** upon a written request from a client. At Children's Hope, and increasingly at other agencies, we normally provide a copy to our clients. We believe it is important for them to know what was written about them. However, if a homestudy is disapproved, we reserve the right to keep the study confidential although we will provide the family with a letter stating our reasons for the denial. Families have a right to know in writing, why they were denied approval. Agencies need to justify their denial with hard evidence; the decision cannot be made capriciously.

After the homestudy is reviewed our families receive notice of the committee's decision. Most parents are approved. However, if one is disapproved he has the right to be told the specific reasons for the disapproval and if the disapproval is permanent or conditional.

Those who are disapproved are usually individuals the social service worker and Adoption Review Committee feel to have a home situation that is unstable or, at best, highly questionable. Of course, this is a subjective determination and the disapproved client would probably not agree. Because of the subjective nature of the homestudy determination, Children's Hope may require a psychological evaluation. The evaluation is a way of confirming or contradicting the decision of the Adoption Review Committee. If the psychological evaluation supports the feelings of the committee, then the committee usually feels it can disapprove with impunity. However, if there is a discrepancy between the committee's feelings and that of the psychological evaluation, then further study is needed.

If a couple (or single parent) is disapproved at our agency, there is an appeal procedure they may use if they feel an unfair decision has been reached. They may appeal directly to the director of the agency who will then impanel a review board consisting of the agency director and two members of the Board of Directors (members of the community and not staff persons of the agency). They will review the findings of the Adoption Review Committee and request the couple (or single parent) to come before them and answer the concerns of the committee. This panel will then decide whether another homestudy should be done. If the decision is "no," then the matter is finished. However, if the decision is that another study is needed, then an independent social worker is retained to do the new study. All the expense incurred for the new study is borne by Children's Hope, and the new study completely replaces the previous study. If the new study recommends approval the family is approved. If it recommends disapproval, the matter is settled. A couple (or single parent) is permitted only one appeal, and will not be allowed to appeal the finding of the second (replacement) homestudy.

If an agency doesn't have an appeals process, you should first check with the agency director. If that doesn't work, contact the agency's state licensing consultant and express your concerns. Ask him if you have any recourse.

ACCEPTING A HOMESTUDY DONE BY ANOTHER AGENCY— UPDATES AND ADDENDUMS

An agency may or may not accept a homestudy which was done by another licensed agency if the homestudy is not too old (Immigration requires a homestudy to be within one year). However, they will usually require an **update**, which means a worker will visit the family for a number of visits and put the study in a written form which the agency is accustomed to using. There will be a cost for this service which will vary depending on the agency. It may range from less than half the cost of the first homestudy to the full fee the agency charges for a homestudy. The agency will only update a homestudy done by another agency if the original study is fairly recent. The amount of time which is considered too old will be determined by the new agency (usually 1-2 years). The significant thing is that the family situation is appreciably the same and nothing much has changed since the first study was done. If the family situation has significantly changed, or if the agency feels the first study is too old, it will require a new homestudy be conducted.

What if you change your mind about the type of child you are willing to accept or want your homestudy to reflect some other idea not stated in the original study? In that case, your agency will usually do an **addendum**. It is unlikely an agency will do an addendum on a homestudy done by another agency. But, if the agency did the original study, they will likely do an addendum. The cost should not be significant. However, just because the agency did the original study does not guarantee they will do an addendum. The agency may feel an addendum is not appropriate if the family is now requesting a different type (i.e. special needs, American vrs. foreign, etc.) or age of child. They may want to investigate the impact upon the family and how the family dynamics will change with the addition of this child. The agency may then insist on an update or even a completely new study.

If you decide to adopt again, you will, at least, be required to have your homestudy updated. The reason is that now your family situation is substantially changed with the addition of your new family member. If more than a year has passed since you adopted, there is a good likelihood your agency will require a new homestudy, even if they did the original.

For readers who would like to see what a completed homestudy looks like, we refer you to Appendix B.

CHAPTER EIGHT

FEES

THE FIRST and easiest thing to say about fees is that they are always climbing! Fees seem to change so fast that, undoubtedly, by the time this edition is published, much of what is said will no longer be accurate. However, in an effort to give the reader an idea of what can be expected in terms of total overseas adoption expense, it is necessary to talk about fees. Therefore, what we can say is that, by the publication date of this edition, these fees were in effect for Children's Hope Adoption Services (only one of many programs) but one would need to contact a particular program to know what fees apply **TODAY**.

An overseas adoption through Children's Hope, at the time of publication, will cost prospective parents between four and ten thousand dollars, with an average cost of about eight thousand dollars. That is all-inclusive and covers agency expenses, overseas cost and travel.

"Why must it cost so much money for an overseas adoption?"

That is a question we are often asked. At Children's Hope we answer by saying that we are not a church, or state supported entity, nor do we receive government subsidies. Our program is paid for by fees for service. Like most organizations the income of the agency must be sufficient to cover normal operating costs — rent, utilities, salaries of the workers, supplies, equipment, etc., as well as to provide enough revenue to cover the periodic emergency.

The cost for an overseas adoption through Children's Hope are divided between money that goes directly to the agency and that which goes overseas, termed the "Overseas Program Expense." Since Children's Hope works with many different programs in several different countries, the Overseas Program Expense will be different for each program. ALL of that expense goes to the foreign source and does not provide revenue to Children's Hope. The Overseas Program Fee pays overseas attorneys, foreign representatives, orphanage donations, translations, etc. — all overseas.

In Michigan, the fees charged by Children's Hope (as well as all other agencies) must be filed and approved by Michigan Probate Court in the various counties in which we work. Currently, the following fee structure applies. It should be noted that, like most adoption program literature, ours frequently contains the provision: **ALL FEES ARE SUBJECT TO CHANGE WITHOUT NOTICE**. Furthermore, we quote Children's Hope fees here only to provide an example. Obviously any other program will have a somewhat different fee schedule.

FEES PAYABLE TO CHILDREN'S HOPE FOR INTERNATIONAL ADOPTIONS THROUGHOUT THE ADOPTION PROCESS

Phase I — The Application

The Inquiry Letter and Response

The process of becoming a Children's Hope Client is usually initiated by sending a letter requesting information. Children's Hope responds by sending a form letter which explains our current available programs, some promotional literature such as recent newspaper articles, and a formal application for adoption. The response letter, like the *Children's Hope Handbook*, is always being updated to reflect the current status of Children's Hope with respect to adoption sources and the process of adoption.

If the family is interested in pursuing an adoption with our help they will return the completed application form with a $50 non-refundable fee. This fee covers an initial screening of the application and payment for the information packet which contains the *Children's Hope Handbook* and additional reading material.

Application and Reading Packet $50

The reading packet contains relevant literature on adoption and the material included is always being updated and improved. We mail the reading packet to inform the prospective parent on all aspects of our program as well as to provide general information on international adoption. This allows the parent to make an informed decision whether or not to continue with plans to pursue an international adoption through our agency. If their decision is "yes, they want to continue," they return a form requesting a formal meeting with agency staff.

Formal Assessment/Orientation Interview Fee $200

This fee covers a two-hour interview where the needs and desires of the prospective adoptive parents are explored and the feasibility of finding a suitable child is discussed. It is also the time when the various options of the Children's Hope Program are presented—the different countries from which we are currently working, the programs, waiting times, etc. During this interview, the risks associated with an international adoption are explained and at the conclusion of the session we ask the clients to sign a "Statement of Understanding." This statement indicates the risks have been explained and the clients are proceeding as mature adults, aware that this is an imperfect system and anything can go wrong.

Based upon the interview a preliminary determination is made as to whether or not Children's Hope will be able to assist the family in finding the type of child they desire. Formal acceptance, however, will be contingent upon an approved homestudy and favorable psychological evaluation (if a psychological evaluation should be required).

The Homestudy Fee $900

Children's Hope charges a fee of nine hundred dollars to conduct a formal homestudy. This fee covers the social work expenses—travel, salary, costs to prepare documents, etc. At our agency the fee is payable in two parts, $500 when the homestudy is begun, and $400 upon completion. If for some reason it is determined the prospective applicants will not receive an "approved status" for their homestudy, they have the option of not completing the study and the second payment is never required. This gives the client a way to exit without actually having received a "disapproval" and also a means of saving some of his money. Once the homestudy process is started, the fee for the first part is nonrefundable.

Psychological Evaluation

This is, technically, not an agency expense. Children's Hope sometimes requires a favorable psychological determination for clients wishing to adopt. Some countries in which we work also have this requirement. For those clients required to have psychological testing, they can expect to spend between $200 - $600 for this service.

The successful completion of phase I results in formal acceptance into the Children's Hope program.

Phase II — Agency Processing Fee $700 or $300

Children's Hope charges a $300 processing fee for an interstate or domestic placement, and $700 for an international placement. This fee is payable after the homestudy is approved, the applicants receive a favorable psychological examination, and are ready to begin preparing their foreign dossier. The fee covers the cost of:

(1) Communicating with the client regarding the adoption plans, as well as communicating with the program or international source regarding the child's adoption.

(2) Reviewing and assembling the documents and seeing that a formalized set gets to the proper program.

(3) Contacting the Immigration and Naturalization Service on the client's behalf.

(4) Receiving and reviewing documents on the referral and forwarding them to the client.

(5) Assisting the client in making arrangements for the overseas stay and assuring there is someone to meet the client while in a foreign country.

(6) Preparing documents for the Interstate Compact Office, if necessary.

(7) Preparing a set of documents for the client to take personally when traveling overseas to get his/her child.

(8) Paying for administrative expenses as well as agency overhead, including telephone calls, telex, utilities, rent, etc.

(9) The expense involved in the upkeep of the client's file necessary to meet state legal and licensing requirements.

International Program Fee

Children's Hope International Program Fees are set by the individuals or organizations overseas responsible for placing the child. The entire fee goes directly to the foreign source and, of that fee, Children's Hope receives no portion. This fee reflects the expense incurred on behalf of the child, birthmother, and the completion of the adoption abroad. Although each country has different regulations and procedures, in all successful adoptions many people overseas have expended time, effort, and expertise (often at personal risk); they deserve to be compensated for their efforts.

Current International Program Fees for Children's Hope Programs

1. Colombia (Bienestar). Technically there is no program fee as such, but adoptive parents will be responsible for legal assistance and translations. Prospective parents should plan to have at least $1,000 set aside to cover these expenses.

2. Honduras — $4,000 - $5,000, depending upon which program or individual attorney with which we work. In addition, parents may be responsible for foster care ($200 per month) until completion of the adoption and medical expenses for the child.

3. Guatemala — $4,100. In addition, parents are responsible for foster care until completion of the adoption and medical expenses which the child may incur.

4. Chile — $5,000 - $6,500, depending on age of child at time of referral (it is more expensive for a newborn). Parents must also have their formal adoption dossier translated in advance before submission to Chile. The average translation cost is $350.

5. Paraguay — $4,000. This fee includes foster care.

Phase III — Post-Placement Services (When Supervision Is By Children's Hope Adoption Services)

When adoption is finalized overseas $200.

When adoption is finalized through Michigan Courts (readoption or guardianship) $600.

Post-placement services involve steps necessary for achieving citizenship for the child and preparing post-placement reports to send to the child's birth country and courts. If the client is adopting through Michigan Probate Court, supervisory visits will be made and reports submitted to the court until the Order of Adoption is obtained.

During the post-placement period, reports and photographs of the family and child will be sent to the overseas source from which the child came. It is very important to send this information to foreign programs and courts. The people in these countries are obviously interested in what happens to the children they place for adoption. It is a courtesy to keep them informed and it helps assure that other families in the future will also be able to adopt from that country. It is one of the few things the agency can do to help foster a more positive image of adoption overseas. **This is very important if people are going to continue to adopt internationally.**

Additional fees for which prospective parents will be asked to be responsible include:

•Foreign adoption decree and court transcripts, when not provided in English, will need to be translated at about $15 per page.

•Notarizations, verifications, authentications (fees differ with the number of documents and the fees of each foreign consulate).

•Medical examinations for adoptive parents and fees for passports.

•I-600A filing fee for U.S. Immigration ($50).

•Program fees for cooperating or networking programs, i.e., Los Ninos International, LIMIAR, programs in other states etc., (each program has its own program fee which covers the cost of legal, medical, and child care expenses). If a person is working with Children's Hope and a networking program, they pay only the International Program Fee of the networking program. Although they would have agency fees for both agencies involved, they would have only one International Program Fee.

•Travel and hotel expenses (or escort fees) which will differ with each country because of distance and type of accommodations.

•U.S. visa fee for each child to be brought to the United States ($150) as well as fees for photographic services, your child's medical examination and other incidentals.

•Filing fees for probate court (usually around $15, but varies depending on which court) if you are adopting or readopting in your state of residence. Legal fees if your court requires you to have legal representation.

ALL FEES, WAITING TIMES, AND SPECIFIC REQUIREMENTS ARE SUBJECT TO CHANGE

Conclusion

Adoption is expensive. Unfortunately, the way international adoptions are structured today and the necessary expenses involved preclude lower income families from this alternative. Perhaps some day Congress will pass legislation to financially assist such families. In the meantime, certain agencies (**Americans for International Aid and Adoption, Bethany Christians Services, Adoption Services of WACAP,** and others) have "scholarship" or low interest loan funds or payment plans available for the adoption of "special needs children."

When you think of spending four to ten thousand dollars for an adoption, it seems like a great deal of money. Perhaps a way to keep it in perspective would be to compare the international adoption expense with the cost of having a baby in a hospital. At our community hospital in Mt. Pleasant, Michigan, the expenses for an uncomplicated vaginal delivery with a two or three day hospital stay are $2,800. If the baby was delivered by Cesarean section and the mother required a five day stay in the hospital, the cost would be $3,400. In addition, the mother would incur obstetrical charges of $700 - $800, pre-natal care expenses of $250 and anesthesia charges of $400. A woman having a baby in our community could expect to spend approximately $4,000 (if there were no problems).

Many national companies have **"Adoption Benefit Plans"** to help pay some of the cost of an adoption. With the right information, a person might approach his/her employer and see whether they would be receptive to such a program. To get a copy of a brochure explaining the programs already in existence, write to the National Adoption Exchange and request their publication, *"Adoption Benefit Plans: Corporate Response to a Changing Society."* The address is:

> **National Adoption Exchange**
> 1218 Chestnut Street
> Philadelphia, PA 19107

We frequently hear from clients, "There are so many other things I could do with that money." This is undoubtedly true. For $20,000 you could install a tennis court. You could put vinyl siding on your house for about $6,500; take a 38 day cruise to the South Pacific for $12,970; or buy a new Cheverolet Beretta for $10,598.

It's a question of priorities!

CHAPTER NINE

WAITING FOR YOUR REFERRAL

The Formal Wait

AT CHILDREN'S HOPE, we are often asked, "how long a period of time can I expect to wait?"

Our response is: "From the time your documents get to (wherever they are going) you can expect a wait of about . . . (each program is different)."

For us, **the clock starts running from the day the official adoption dossier is submitted overseas.** We call this period of time, "the formal wait." It is a difficult time for prospective parents, because previously they had been busy gathering documents, having their homestudy conducted, and generally keeping busy. Now it seems there is nothing to do, but wait.

In the spring of 1987 we received an interesting mailing from the International Concerns Committee for Children in Colorado. The piece was written by Deborah McCurdy and was directed at parents who were in this stage of the adoption process. The article entitled *"How to Make the Wait for Your Child Easier to Bear,"* is excellent advice for all prospective parents and we produce it here, with permission of the author. This article is **NOT** copyrighted and **may be reprinted without permission.**

HOW TO MAKE THE WAIT FOR YOUR CHILD EASIER TO BEAR
by Deborah McCurdy

(Reprinted from an International Concerns Committee for Children publication — ICCC, 911 Cypress Drive, Boulder, CO 80303)

When your home study is approved by your local adoption agency and your documents are mailed to your chosen placement agency, you may go through a difficult time. Most adoptive parents start out with a mixture of eager anticipation and fear that something will go wrong.

For many people, hope tends to give way to discouragement and occasional despair as the wait lengthens. Even after your child is chosen for you, you may feel depressed and anxious because he must remain in the care of other people until pre-adoption procedures are completed. There is often an intense feeling of frustration at not being able to control the adoption process personally. Since I have experienced these feelings myself and have seen them often in other adoptive parents, I offer the following suggestions to help you endure the wait. (You may want to post them where you'll see them often!)

Expect some frustrations and delays as a normal part of the adoption process. This applies whether you are working with a U.S.-based agency or a foreign source. There is really no way of accurately predicting how long you will wait for your child. Placement agencies give estimates—often with reluctance—since adoptive parents expect this. However, these estimates are only educated guesses, or projections based on how long people have waited who applied some time ago and are now receiving their children. Unfortunately, even the most promising adoption programs can encounter unexpected setbacks at any time during the wait. There may be delays due to changes in regulations, slowdowns in the courts, a marked increase in applicants, or the introduction of new procedures. Ask the placement agency for the probably maximum wait they would anticipate and focus on that time and beyond, rather than expecting the shortest possible time. Curiously, the wait should prove somewhat easier if you expect it to be a long one (while realizing that you might be pleasantly surprised).

Don't fight your hope. Discouragement is especially common in those who have had past disappointments in trying to conceive or adopt. Something seems to happen during the wait that I call "fighting hope." The adoptive parents may start out with confidence that the adoption will work out fairly quickly and easily. Then the delays and frustrations that are common in adoption come their way. Whether or not a child has been assigned, the parents start to despair. In some cases, it seems as though they are trying to protect themselves from another disappointment by **refusing to let themselves hope** that the adoption will work out. If you find yourself becoming angry and pessimistic, or if you begin to feel that you will never get your child, ask yourself if you could be fighting and defeating your own hope. Then remind yourself that delays are normal, and that nothing can stop you from adopting eventually if you refuse to give up!

Think of your placement agency as a gate through the wall of paperwork and procedures that separate you from your child—rather than as a part of that wall. Although the agency is **enabling** you to obtain your child, anxiety causes some waiting parents to perceive the agency in the opposite way—as part of the system **keeping them from** their child. When this happens, the parents' criticisms or complaints can hurt the agency staff and create antagonism. It is very natural for people to be angry when parenthood has already been delayed through infertility, so anger felt toward the placement agency (because of further delays) may be misdirected. Placement agencies work very hard with our own authorities and foreign courts to expedite each adoption, since the process is a complex one. It is often impossible to communicate clearly the reasons for delays or complications over barriers of distance, language, and culture. Dedicated agency directors generally make tremendous sacrifices of their own time and resources to keep their programs going despite unexpected changes in regulations or procedures in foreign countries. When you experience disappointment, your pain is their pain. They get discouraged too; they need your understanding and patience. It is not unusual for parents to feel at times that their agency let them down, no matter what agency they have chosen. However, it helps a lot if you can understand that delays and setbacks are beyond the agency's control — and often beyond anyone's control.

Stay committed to your agency — and your child. Once parents have carefully selected a placement agency, they need to trust it to do its best to arrange their child's adoption on its own. Their understandable desire to be in control needs to be suspended for a time. The agency and its foreign representatives are the ones that are closest to the situation: parents need to let them determine what can and cannot be done to expedite the adoption. For instance, the agency cannot pressure its overseas representative or the foreign court to speed things up; in most countries this is counter productive. Nor can the agency insist on the frequent progress reports from overseas that parents would love to have. (Short-staffed foreign agencies and adoption facilitators generally need to direct their energies to caring for many children and processing as many adoptions as possible.)

Once you accept a particular child (after receiving whatever limited medical information is available), think of that child as yours, just as if he or she had been born to you. The agency cannot guarantee that the child will arrive free of problems — any more than an obstetrician can guarantee that any baby will be born free of birth defects or a difficult personality. Becoming a parent involves taking these risks. Once the legal process is under way to make the child yours, you and the agency have both made a commitment. Parents are expected to honor this commitment unless the child turns out to have a serious problem that they cannot handle. Similarly, the agency commits itself to doing everything in its power to complete an adoption — although parents must prepare themselves for the possibility of losing the first child that is assigned to them.

Because of unexpected delays, a child may arrive months older than the parents had planned on. Some parents worry about this so much that they may be tempted to withdraw from the adoption. However, research has shown that most children make an excellent adjustment to loving adoptive parents, given time and patience, even though they may have originally bonded to someone else. It is encouraging to read OURS Magazine (available for $16 a year from OURS, Inc., 3307 Highway 100 North, Minneapolis, MN 55422). Here you will find pictures of beautiful smiling children with stories of the trials that their adoptive parents went through before they came. The happy ending is there for all to see!

Discuss your feelings with your local agency and with those who have adopted. Your local home study agency, which often is not the agency handling the placement, may be a good resource for helping you endure the wait. (You may feel more free to vent your anger and frustration at the process in the presence of a social worker who knows you well and is not an employee of the agency processing your adoption.) If your home study agency is also serving as your placement agency, you can certainly express your concerns and your distress while clarifying to the agency staff that you are not blaming them for delays or disappointments over which they have no control. If you feel an impulse to withdraw from your adoption, explore this with your social worker. It may represent a desperate attempt to take control and end the uncertainty and sense of powerlessness that go with your situation. It may help a lot to talk to other adoptive parents who have successfully weathered a difficult wait. Locate a local adoptive parents group; its members will support you.

Give yourself some enjoyable new projects to take your mind off your worries. Furnish the nursery, study Spanish from cassettes, and do something entirely unrelated to the adoption. Choose things that are fun to do together that you may not have time for after the baby comes. If you take a second honeymoon, be sure to let the placement agency know the dates you'll be away and your vacation phone numbers.

Think about what you'd do if the worst possible thing happened. First of all, what **is** the worst possible outcome? At our lowest ebb, we imagine that we might not get our child at all. However, I do not think that this is a realistic fear. In twelve years of working in intercountry adoption, I have never known any adoptive parents with an approved home study who did not eventually get a child — provided that they did not give up. Some had to change programs or countries when their first choice of source unexpectedly closed, but all who trusted the adoption **process**, and stayed with it, eventually succeeded! So what **is** the worst thing that could happen? Unfortunately, a child chosen for you could possibly become very sick or even die; this is rare, in my experience. Or the child could become unavailable for some other reason, such as a birth-mother's changing her mind before her parental rights were terminated in court. What would you do then? Naturally you would grieve for a time, but as soon as you felt ready to proceed, the placement agency would ordinarily give you preference for the next suitable child. Years ago my husband and I lost the first baby assigned to us, but the wonderful little boy who came to us later is so much a part of our family that we can't imagine any other child in his place. Other parents in our situation tell us the same thing. So don't give up; be patient and persistent. Tell yourself that when you do finally get your child—when, not if—all that you have gone through to become parents will seem well worth the struggle!

(First published in 1987 by the International Concerns Committee for Children)

One Additional Suggestion— Collect Orphanage Donations

Another suggestion is to use the time to collect donations for the orphanage, program, or country with which you are working. All programs need a constant supply of baby bottles and nipples, diapers, blankets, shirts, gowns, etc. Even if your child was in foster care, there is **ALWAYS** an orphanage in the city which needs your supplies. **Bringing donations with you is an extra measure of goodwill.** Good used baby things are all right. Your parent support group will also help you collect these items. You won't have any trouble getting enough, the problem will be what to do with all the extra that doesn't fit in your luggage! The solution is to leave the items with your agency so that the traveling parent can transport them. You can also send extra materials to some of the needy groups listed in *OURS Magazine*.

THE REFERRAL

In most cases the initial agency referral will be by telephone. You will be given basic information regarding the child: age, sex, country of origin or ethnic background and health status. If the child has any known health problems at the time of referral, you will be informed of this. You are requested to make your decision regarding a child offering as soon as possible. This does not allow much time for such an important decision, so it is important that you thoroughly explore during the homestudy process the types of children you are best prepared to parent. A referral can happen any time after the approval of your homestudy—whenever it does happen you will probably NOT be expecting it. Prepare yourself by carefully considering in advance all the possible options and deciding which type of child would or would not be appropriate for you. If you decide you cannot accept a particular referral, it is important that your agency know as soon as possible so they will have time to find another family for the child.

Should you decide that you wish to accept a particular referral, your agency will notify the foreign source and your documents will be presented to the program or attorney in charge of your child overseas. At the same time, photographs and medical information on the child will be sent to you via your agency. Ideally, you should be periodically contacted and kept informed of the progress of your child as well as the adoptive process. Usually, however, you will not receive a progress report unless the child becomes ill.

When you do receive and accept a referral for a child you may be asked to sign an agency referral agreement, indicating what is known about the child as well as the expenses involved. **Even though you have signed this agreement, you should regard the referral as TENTATIVE until you are actually ready to travel for your child.** The reason for this is that until you get on the plane for home, **things can still go wrong** which might prevent the placement. Everything possible will be done to insure that each referral ends in an adoption. Occasionally, events occur which make this impossible, however; birthmothers can legally change their minds at various points in the process, orphanage directors can change their minds, government policies may change, etc. Even when your referral remains intact, the actual court process in the foreign country can be prolonged due to unforeseen complications. It is best to tell as few people about your referral as possible during this stressful phase of your adoption. Believe us, you will get tired of explaining to people over and over again why your adoption is taking longer than anticipated. Friends and acquaintances, with the best of intentions, will begin to raise doubts about the successful completion of your child's adoption. They will ask questions which you probably won't be able to answer. To avoid unnecessary stress and frustration, tell only close friends and family members and explain that you wish to keep this a private matter until the child is ready to join you.

CHAPTER TEN

RECEIVING YOUR CHILD—
YOUR TRIP OVERSEAS

YOUR TRIP overseas to meet your child should be one of the highlights of your life. As soon as you leave the airplane in your foreign destination, your adventure begins. New smells, sounds and sights assault you on all sides and remind you that you have left the security of the familiar and have entered a strange and exotic land.

At Children's Hope we provide an itinerary and personal instruction sheet for each of our clients. They are met at the airport by our English speaking representative and immediately made to feel both expected and welcome. This is the apex of a long and difficult process and we feel it is extremely important this be a positive experience.

FOREIGN CURRENCY

One of the first things we advise you to do is to change a small amount of money into foreign currency. You only need enough to pay for little things such as taxi fares, meals, and souvenirs. This can usually be done at the Miami airport which serves as a hub for flights to Latin America. In most foreign countries the rate of exchange for currency is not one for one. For example, recently in Guatemala, the rate of exchange was three of the Guatemala quetzales for one U.S. dollar. Say, for example, your fare for a taxi trip came to twenty quetzales. If you didn't have local currency, the taxi driver would (as a favor to a new tourist) permit you to pay in dollars. He would tell you that a dollar is equivalent to roughly, one quetzal (which it officially might be). By paying in dollars, however, you have paid about three times what the fare would have been if you had changed some money and paid in quetzales. Once you are in the country of your destination you can go to a bank or official money-changing enterprise to have larger sums of money changed. Change your money only with those who are specifically authorized to change money. Be sure not to trade money on the street, no matter what rate of exchange you are being offered. This is a hazardous enterprise; the money you buy could be counterfeit or the person you are buying from could be an undercover agent and you will be arrested. Also, try and not change more money than you will actually need. In some cases you will not be able to change the currency back to U.S. dollars when you leave the country.

TOURIST CARD

When you embark on your journey you will need to purchase a tourist card. The expense for this is minimal. The tourist card will have an original and a copy. It is important to remember that the original will be handed in to foreign immigration officials when you enter the country and the copy surrendered when you leave. You should try and keep the copy in a safe place, such as with your passport. If you lose the copy, you will be required to fill out a new card before you are allowed to board the airplane for your flight home.

CUSTOMS

Upon arrival at your destination you will need to go through a customs inspection. This is a routine procedure but may be far more restrictive than you have ever experienced in the United States or on previous trips abroad. Customs officials will probably request you to open your luggage and unpack it for inspection. If your are carrying an extra suitcase filled with new items such as presents or orphanage donations, custom officials may assume they are intended for **resale** and could tax you for them. In order to avoid this possibility it is a good idea not to pack items in their original wrappers and remove all sales receipts. Therefore, these things all appear to be "used" and no one will care whether or not you bring them into the country without paying tax. If they are donation goods, a signed and notarized letter from your agency should state the purpose for which the items are intended to be used. Be sure to itemize the items on the letter or they may make you do it in the airport. Remain calm, polite, and smile frequently. You will get through customs quickly.

YOUR TRIP FROM THE AIRPORT AND RECEIVING YOUR BABY

At Children's Hope, our clients who are personally met at the airport are driven in the car of our representative either to the representative's home (most of our clients choose to stay with our representative's family) or a hotel. Other programs probably work differently and it will be necessary for many to take a taxi. If so, one should already have exchanged currency to pay for this expense as previously mentioned.

You will probably receive your child either that evening or the following morning. This will be one of those indelible moments in time which will always remain with you.

YOUR FIRST EMBASSY CONTACT

Shortly after you arrive in the foreign country you will need to go to the U.S. Consulate and present to Consulate officials form I-171H "Notice of Favorable Determination Concerning Application for Advance Processing of Orphan Petition" (if you are adopting in the country) or, form I-171 "Notice of Approval of Relative Immigrant Visa Petition" (if you are getting a guardianship and adopting in your state of residence). These forms indicate to your overseas consulate that your advance processing (I-600A) received a favorable determination. **You should do this early, even if you are planning a stay of weeks.** Although they should have a copy of this on file, sometimes they misplace their copy. If you are missing a document or if they misplaced the cable of the I-171H you have plenty of time to call home and have your agency send you the needed document or have INS recable the consulate.

If you are traveling to Latin America to receive your child under a guardianship, you may need to present proof that you have met your state's preadoption requirements.

While at the embassy, you will receive materials pertaining to your adopted child and make an appointment to obtain your child's visa at a later date. Included in the material you receive will be a list of approved physicians, one of whom you will chose to conduct a physical examination on your child. There will also be instructions to follow and additional forms pertaining to the **orphan petition** (form I-600) which you had received earlier, but which you will now be able to complete and turn in to the consulate when you apply for your child's visa.

YOUR CHILD'S FOREIGN PASSPORT

If you are fortunate, the passport issued by the foreign government on your child will already have been secured for you before your arrival. We always try to accomplish this for our clients at Children's Hope, because waiting to get a foreign passport can be a terribly frustrating experience with long delays and many disappointments. We have heard stories from people who have waited for days in foreign passport offices waiting for passports which were lost or incomplete. In fairness to the foreign country, you could not obtain a U.S. passport in three days! Adoptive parents are impatient for positive results and get angry when those results don't occur as expected. This is one reason North Americans are perceived of as "pushy" by most Latin Americans.

It would be a good idea for all clients to ask their agency if the passport on their child has been secured in advance of their travel. It can literally make the difference between a wonderful experience and one of extreme frustration.

Of course, this does not apply in all cases or all countries. For example in Honduras, where the parents go to **INITIATE** the adoption, the parent or agency cannot apply for the passport until the adoption is completed, some two or three months after the parents have left Honduras.

THE MEDICAL EXAMINATION

The overseas medical examination is not extensive by U.S. standards. Rather, it is simple and the primary purpose is to inform the consulate whether or not the child has any infectious disease or medical condition which would bar his/her entrance into the United States (i.e. mental disorder, tuberculosis, contagious disease). **The criteria used to determine whether or not a child will be allowed entrance is for immigration purposes only and it is not meant to be a thorough medical evaluation.** Many minor physical conditions the child may have (undernutrition, skin disorders, lice, etc.) might not even be mentioned to the adopting parents. Therefore it is an extremely wise decision to have the child reexamined once the child arrives home. If you have serious doubts about the child's health, ask for a more thorough exam or take the child to an embassy recommended pediatrician for a second opinion.

The doctor will present the parent (usually the day following the examination) with a sealed envelope to give to the U.S. Consulate officials at the parents' visa appointment. This will inform the Consulate as to the child's health status for immigration purposes.

COURTESY AND MANNERS IN A FOREIGN COUNTRY

When you are in a foreign country, you are an ambassador for the United States. How you look and behave affects the way the native citizens of that country regard North Americans and, in particular, the image they have of adoptive parents. It is important to remember that you are a guest in the country and just as you would expect a guest to behave appropriately in your home, you should try to do likewise.

Citizens in other countries have many misconceptions and stereotypes of North Americans. We often hear that North Americans are "demanding," "have money to burn," "are rude and insensitive," etc. (see insert, how Colombians perceive North Americans). These stereotypes are developed because of communication problems and cultural differences. Still, through polite and thoughtful behavior, such myths can be dispelled.

At Children's Hope we try to prepare our clients who are going overseas by providing handouts concerning the culture of the country from which they will adopt. The following illustration is from a handout we have used concerning Colombia. To be honest, we don't know where this material originally was developed. It was provided to us by a Peace Corps worker who had been stationed in Colombia about ten years ago. The names on the handout indicating authorship are Sr. Herman Perez of Bavaria, S.A. and Sr. Sam Modello of Universidad Javeriana. We have found this material useful and continue to provide it to our clients who are going to Colombia to adopt a child. We reproduce a portion of it here for the purpose of illustration and to show why Colombians can easily misinterpret the behaviors of North Americans.

In Colombia you will find that all levels of society follow an almost ritualistic formula in the phrases and when to use them will help to create an "ambiente" which will greatly facilitate your work. . . . Thinking of these phrases in terms of their equivalent English meaning or in terms to which we are accustomed can often create problems. A Colombian in a hurry will think nothing of stopping to greet you, ask about your health, your family, etc. On the other hand a North American will give a quick "Hi" and be on his way. Often too, because of our "hurry up" mentality, we may feel that the Colombian is being insincere, yet **your** curt "Hi" gives the impression that you are unfriendly. . . .

In meeting someone you are acquainted with in the street, and you do not wish to be detained, but you do wish to greet him/her, it is the custom to say only: "Adiós".

If it is someone you know fairly well, you can say: "Adiós Carlos, como estás" or "Adiós Carlos, como te va?"

(When making introductions) the man does not wait for the woman to extend her hand because it is the custom for the woman to shake hands at all times. It is also the custom for the person making the introduction to give both names. . . .

Some persons because of their age or position demand certain respect. They often prefer that you use their first name rather than their last name, but it must always be preceded by "Don" or "Doña" as follows:

"Come está, don Manuel? — "Como está, doña María?"

In these cases it is always safe to use "Señor" or "Señora" or follow the lead of your Colombian friends.

In the case of someone who has a professional title, the last name is usually preceded by "Doctor" — "Doctor Rodrígues."

The lower class and the campesinos often refer to people of the upper classes as "Doctor"; so don't be surprised if you are addressed in this manner.

In most Latin American countries you will find that almost anyone that has a college degree of any kind is referred to as "Doctor."[1]

How Colombian High School Students Perceive of North Americans[2]

1. They feel superior and bossy.
2. They feel people of different races are inferior.
3. They plan to cheat in business.

---

1. Herman Pérez and Sam Modello, "Customs of Courtesy Most Commonly Used in Colombia," Handout originally provided Peace Corps Workers in 1977. A photocopy of this was given to us by a former client to assist other parents adopting from Colombia to understand the Colombian culture.

2. Susan Hammonds. Part of the material on Colombia which was part of the Peace Corp packet. This was a survey of the opinions of high school students in a Colombian School.

4. They are afraid of meeting the "wrong kind of people."
5. They are easily cheated in terms of prices in Colombia.
6. They think they are the only ones who are Americans.
7. They feel Colombians are not civilized yet.
8. They don't care about people's social position.
9. They stay with their own group.
10. The girls wear more make-up at an earlier age.
11. The hair is worn longer.
12. Their pace of life is very fast.
13. When making a request they go straight to the point, and receive an answer in the same way.
14. They wear blue jeans a lot.
15. They obey and enforce laws.
16. They like animals more.
17. They aren't willing to learn Spanish (some).
18. They have many religions.
19. They are not polite.
20. They are good athletes.
21. They are sloppy.
22. They are independent.
23. More of them are Protestant.
24. The girls are more open.

What Colombian High School Students Believe North Americans Think of Colombians

1. They enjoy bullfighting.
2. They are not exact about time.
3. They have a dirty country.
4. They are a very critical people.
5. They are clean and elegant.
6. They dress very well.
7. The streets are full of litter.
8. The food is cheaper.
9. The people are friendly.
10. They are critical of North Americans.
11. They drive dangerously.
12. They have a guard outside their homes.
13. They like soccer.
14. In large groups they all talk at once.

15. They can carry 2 or 3 conversations at a time.
16. They are very polite.
17. They don't follow laws.
18. They are interested in politics.
19. Their greetings are much more effusive.
20. They are smaller physically.
21. The upper class people are prejudiced against Indians and lower class people.
22. They are stubborn.
23. They copy ideas.
24. They don't like Gringos.

TAKING CARE OF YOUR NEW CHILD OVERSEAS

Once you are handed your baby (or introduced to your older child) overseas, that child becomes your responsibility. In every way, you are now the "real" (and legal) parent. You should be prepared to assume these responsibilities from the moment you take possession of the child.

You will need to either bring from the United States or purchase abroad travel clothing (including diapers), shoes, and toiletries for your child. If a baby, be sure not to change the kind of formula your baby has been using until you return home. Changing a baby's formula can cause stomach disturbance and diarrhea. You have enough to worry about while you are overseas without adding this to the agenda.

Ask your agency for the name of a family who has recently traveled for up-to-date advice on prices and what other things to expect. It may be worthwhile to pack some of the new extremely flat disposable diapers as they may be quite expensive overseas. Clothing may be very cheap and can be kept as a souvenir. Ask about items like a stroller or baby front or back pack. This can be a life-saver if you plan to do any tourist activities, or in those long walkways you will find at the airport.

Just as you need to provide clothing, you should also plan in advance to bring certain medications, such as diaper ointment or Kwell (in the event of lice). It should be noted, however, that these things can usually be purchased overseas and it is not necessary to burden yourself carrying unnecessary supplies. We knew one parent who went to Latin America with twenty rolls of toilet paper in her suitcase—had she asked, we would have explained that toilet paper is readily available in every country from which we work!

TAKING CARE OF YOURSELF WHILE VISITING A FOREIGN COUNTRY— FOOD AND DRINK

Besides worrying about the child's health status, you should insure steps to protect your own health. This begins at home and you should already have checked to see whether or not your health insurance will cover you while you are in a foreign country. If not, you can obtain low cost travel insurance for this purpose. You should also have notified your insurance carrier and informed them of the impending adoption and asked when coverage begins for the child.

You have probably heard expressions like "Montezuma's Revenge," or "The Mexican Two-Step." These refer to diarrhea which can be not only debilitating, but can absolutely ruin what would otherwise have been a wonderful adventure.

The diarrhea which a visitor develops while being overseas is sometimes referred to as "traveler's diarrhea." It sounds innocent enough, but diarrhea can range from a minor inconvenience to a life-threatening medical emergency. In almost all cases, however, it comes from either eating improperly prepared food or drinking contaminated water.

The easiest way to avoid such an unpleasant situation is to be careful where and what one eats or drinks. As a visitor your gastrointestinal system will not be accustomed to some of the indigenous bacteria and even if you are careful you may experience some mild disturbance. This is not to impugn the sanitary standards of the country you are in, but merely to indicate that you are **not used to** the bacteria. Like a recent Kaopectate® advertisement depicting a Mexican couple visiting the United States: "hot dogs, apple pie, pizza . . . these things are great, but for diarrhea . . . "

You can minimize your chances for real discomfort by eating only in the best restaurants. Never purchase food such as cervici (a popular seafood dish in most Latin American countries) from roadside vendors. Even at the best restaurants, try and avoid certain foods such as raw salads, milk products or undercooked meat and fish. Peel all fruit **yourself.** Drink only bottled water, and, if that is not available drink carbonated beverages such as colas. Coffee, tea, bottled beer and wine as well as soup should also be acceptable. Many families find it helpful to bring a little 2 or 4 cup plug-in coffee maker or heating coil to put in a cup of water. If you bring one of these you will need an electrical plug adaptor which can be obtained from a travel or luggage store. You can use the boiled water to fix baby's formula, brush your teeth with, etc. If you are staying in a good hotel or private home you can request boiled water.

The Center for Disease Control states that if the water from your tap is too hot to put your hand in comfortably, it is probably safe to drink—if you have no other option. Finally, you can purify water by adding iodine or halazone tablets which are available in kits for travels. Although this method will remove bacteria and **some** parasites, others need to be filtered in order to remove them. Therefore this should be thought of as a method of last resort.

Most of these precautions are just common sense, but the traveler should remind him/herself of the necessity of caution in advance. In the case of gastrointestinal disturbance "an ounce of prevention is worth **MORE** than a pound of cure!"

Be sure to have your agency provide you with the name and address of a reputable physician in the country you are visiting in case of a medical emergency. If this is not possible you can obtain a directory of English-speaking doctors and their fee schedules from the International Association for Medical Assistance to Travelers (IAMAT). Write:

IAMAT
417 Center Street
Lewiston, NY 14092

The doctors listed in this directory are available on a 24 hour basis should you need medical assistance. If you don't have a directory or a list of names, you can contact the U.S. Embassy staff who will provide you with a list of local physicians. If you are taking a prolonged trip (greater than three weeks), plan to visit rural areas, or stay in non-tourist accommodations, you want to read *"Health Information for International Travel—1987,"* put out by the Centers for Disease Control. This may be found in university libraries with a "government depositary" designation, your adoption agency, travel agent, or local health department. If you cannot find a copy, you may purchase one yourself for $4.75. Write to the Superintendent of Documents and request HHS Publication, No. (CDC) 85-8280. The address is:

Superintendent of Documents
U.S. Government Printing Office
Washington, D.C. 20402

YOUR CHILD'S VISA APPOINTMENT

After you have obtained your child's overseas passport and have completed the child's medical examination you will need to return to the

United States Consulate. This will be at a specified time, the appointment you have already made during your first embassy contact. Here, you will deliver to the embassy officials the sealed envelope containing the result of the child's medical examination and the completed forms pertaining to your child's adoption.

All this is necessary so that you may obtain a visa for your child to permit him/her to enter the United States. You may also be interviewed about the adoption and asked some questions regarding the agency or people who assisted you and the amount of money you paid to accomplish the adoption. At this time, you will need to submit the following documents:

1. Form I-600 (Petition to Classify Orphan as an Immediate Relative).
2. Form FS-510 (an application for a visa).
3. The birth certificate for your child.
4. Three photographs of your child. These should be color photographs with a WHITE (not gray or black) background. The instructions you receive from the embassy will give exact specifications on the size of the pictures, as well as the head size of the subject.
5. The decree of adoption, initial and final decrees, or the Agreement of Permanent Guardianship.
6. Certificate of Abandonment by the Court, or the release form of the parent indicating it is an unqualified, irrevocable release of all parental rights.
7. Sealed envelope containing the result of the child's physical examination.
8. Net worth statement of adoptive parents.
9. Letter from employer indicating that one or both parents is gainfully employed.
10. The first page of parent's 1040 federal income tax return.
11. Form I-134, "Affidavit of Support," indicating that the parent assumes full responsibility for financial support for a period of at least 3 years.
12. The Child's foreign passport.
13. Form verifying that state preadoption requirements have been met. This is required by some states and applies to adoptions not finalized abroad or when a family plans to re-adopt in the home state.

14. Visa fee of $150. Check with your agency to see whether the consulate in the country of your destination will accept payment in travelers checks or credit card. Some countries have been known to request adopting parents pay in cash only.

Upon the submission of all these forms and the payment of the U.S. visa fee, the parent(s) will be told to return to the embassy (usually that same afternoon) to receive their child's visa. When they return they will be presented with the visa which will be stamped with a visa symbol. An **IR-4** symbol is used when the adoption process is not yet complete and the parents will be adopting when the child returns home. Parents who receive a Guardianship will receive an IR-4 status. If the adoption has been completed and both parents (or single parent) have traveled to the foreign country an **IR-3** will be stamped. With an IR-3 status, it is not necessary for the parents to adopt in the United States, as the adoption is accepted by federal law as a legal and valid adoption. The parents, however, may chose to readopt in their state of residence (if state law permits) as discussed in Chapter 11.

Upon receipt of the child's visa, parents are usually filled with a feeling of overwhelming joy and relief — now they can leave. They can take their child and go home!

Summary

This has been an explanation of the typical events an adopting parent will encounter overseas and of how Children's Hope assists clients in this aspect of their adoption. **However, each agency will differ in the extent to which it assists clients overseas.** It is important that parents check with their agency to determine what services and assistance will be provided. In some cases parents may be responsible for hiring their own interpreters or guides. When you are at the point in your adoption when travel is imminent, it is wise to ask your agency for the names and telephone numbers of families who have recently traveled and adopted from this country so that you may learn what to expect.

CHAPTER ELEVEN

AFTER YOUR CHILD ARRIVES HOME

WHEN THE FANTASY BECOMES REAL

AFTER PARENTS arrive home with their new child, they are frequently numb. All of the running around, the paper gathering and the chaos is over. The anticipation and expectations have reached fruition and now you are here with this new little person in the family. In most cases, this child is all the adoptive parent ever wanted and everything returns to normal with a minimum of difficulty, though most families will need a period of adjustment.

Sometimes the child does not respond as the parent anticipates and this causes alarm. The child may react negatively, may cry when held or turn its face away from the parent. This can be terribly distressing to the parent, who may feel negative emotions and later guilt for having such feelings. This condition is usually very short-lived.

With an older child the dynamics of adjusting to a new family are quite different than with an infant. There may be a "honeymoon" period which lasts for days or weeks when the child tries to be "good" and the family is fooled as to how easy it all was.

Or, the older adopted child may behave in ways the parent finds embarrassing or inappropriate and the parent may be at a loss to know how to deal with those behaviors. It is not surprising to hear from a new adoptive parent an admission that for a period of time they just "didn't like the child." Such feelings usually disappear in time, but not always. Parents should be aware that there are professional services available should such difficulties arise. It is far better to seek help initially, than to have a disrupted adoption later. This is the time to turn to your social service worker for help.

Studies indicate that the longer a child stays in the pre-adoptive environment, the greater the likelihood for maladjustment and later disruption.[1]

Older children have been "programed" in ways which may seem difficult to understand and make new parents feel extremely uncomfortable. Lying and stealing, acting-out or inappropriate sexual behavior may all be ways in which the child has learned to respond to his/her previous environment. In Latin America, these behaviors may have been effective survival techniques, but in the U.S. they are clearly out of place. Such behaviors present a difficult challenge to new adoptive parents. Parents should be prepared to spend time trying to understand why the child is behaving in this manner and then try to reeducate the child as to what is culturally appropriate. The problem is made more complicated by the language barrier which usually lasts for several months.

When a child behaves in an unpleasant manner it is easiest for the parent to simply become angry and shut-off communication. The parent must learn that the child's behaviors, as unpleasant as they are, are probably the child's way of "reaching out." To become angry or dismiss the child by sending him/her away or resorting to punishment will only serve to exacerbate the problem and further confuse the child as to what is expected. Rather, the child must be taught what behaviors will result in parental approval. This is going to be a slow process and one which will require a great deal of patience. Your social worker and other parents of children adopted at a similar age should be a great help during this time.

Parents may notice their child "smells funny," or at least, "not like we do." Smell is an acute sense and although most people don't realize it, it is an important way we have of distinguishing "same" from "different." (Just observe other mammals and see how important this sense is in the animal kingdom.) To overcome this feeling of difference with your child, wash all of the child's clothing and provide the same toiletries used by the other members of the household. In a brief time this perception will change as the child takes on the characteristic odor (aroma, might be a better word) of the rest of the family.

---

1. Arnold Richard Silverman, "Transracial Adoption in the United States: A Study of Assimilation and Adjustment," Diss. Univ. of Wisconsin, 1986, pp. 226-227.

STILL THINGS TO DO

Just because the child is home does not mean the adoption process is complete — there are still things which must be done.

POST-PLACEMENT SERVICES

Most agencies will require **post-placement services.** These activities consist of the social service worker continuing to meet with the family in order to assist with the child's progress. The worker will prepare periodic reports for the agency as well as reports to be sent overseas to the adoption source. Some foreign agencies will also request written reports from the family.

For those who have finalized their adoption overseas, there is usually no legal obligation to cooperate with this agency requirement. Since the adoption is already finalized the parents could view such an agency "requirement" as illegal and an unwarranted intrusion into their privacy — even if they had previously indicated they would cooperate.

For those who have received a guardianship, cooperating with the agency during the period of post-placement supervision is a legal requirement as the agency has a mandate from the courts to supervise and report to the court.

Yet, whether the parents received an IR-3 or IR-4 visa status and are required, or not required, to cooperate with their agency is not really the issue. **Parents should want to cooperate.**

The adoption authorities in most overseas countries want to be kept informed of the progress of the children whom they are placing for adoption. Overseas sources need to be shown the advantages these children experience as a result of the adoption process. This is readily apparent when one reads post-placement reports which usually shout the happiness families find with the addition of their new child. It goes without saying that **these reports pave the way for other families to follow the same route of international adoption.**

If it is a parent-initiated adoption with minimal agency involvement, there may be no post-placement supervision required. It is a good practice then, for the family to send directly to their foreign lawyer and to the juvenile court judge, two or three letters and pictures in the first year after the adoption. **This will encourage the courts to continue to process adoptions for other families** and certainly will not harm your case if you decide to pursue a second adoption through the same sources later!

The agency's role throughout this process is as a resource to the family. The agency can provide valuable expertise about children from overseas, expectations of parents, naturalization procedures, and other things to be prepared for in the years ahead, based upon the agency's expertise acquired through years of experience.

ADOPTING IN YOUR STATE OF RESIDENCE

Depending on whether you received a guardianship overseas or final adoption decree will determine whether or not you will be adopting or readopting in your state of residence. A guardianship is nothing more than a promise by the parents to adopt the particular child when the child joins them in the United States. Based upon that promise, the foreign court allows the child to leave the country. If you receive a guardianship you will have already stated so on your I-600 petition which indicates that you have met the "pre-adoption requirements" and will be adopting the child when you return home.

If your adoption was finalized overseas and both parents saw the child before or during the adoption process, you will have received a final adoption decree. The United States government recognizes and accepts that decree as valid. It is not technically necessary for you to readopt in the United States as **you already are the legitimate parent.** Some people might like to readopt as a matter of affirmation or for other personal reasons. In some states, **re-adoption may not be allowed, or be allowed only if it is stated in advance of the visa application.** It is important for you to know this information before completing the adoption. Your agency should be knowledgeable in this matter with respect to the laws of your particular state.

If your state permits readoption and this is your desire you should indicate this to your social worker so that she may assist you in obtaining the proper forms for filing with your court. Depending on the state in which you reside, it may or may not be necessary to obtain the services of a lawyer. Some states will permit you to handle your own adoption case, a situation which is referred to as a **pro se adoption** (adopting without a lawyer).

In many states, you may be allowed to change the child's legal age during the adoption proceedings in court. This may be contingent, however, on whether or not the child was abandoned or surrendered. When a child is surrendered, the actual date of birth is known and some courts will be reluctant to change the date. Also, many courts will not change a birth date unless the adjustment is greater than one year. If you want to change the age and birthday, mention this when you are ready to file your adoption petition. Some courts will request a doctor's letter, stating the reasons for the change, such as the child's size, emotional maturity, bone or dental development, etc.

You or your social worker should check with the Clerk of the Court to provide the particular forms as well as general information you will need. These will need to be filed with a stipulated filing fee. If you are representing yourself, you will need to submit a letter to the judge, indicating your reason for wanting to represent yourself.

When your big day arrives you may appear in Court to answer a few questions the Judge may ask. These will be regarding your desire to adopt the child and whether or not you are willing to assume complete responsibility. The judge may also ask you to describe the circumstances of the adoption and ask about the child's health. You should have with you at this time the foreign adoption decree and all other pertinent documents on the child to submit to the judge for inspection. (Your particular situation may be different. Some courts will process the entire adoption through the mail.)

Once you have completed the adoption/readoption process in your state of residence, you can apply for a new state birth certificate. This will usually be mailed to you within a few weeks.

APPLYING FOR NATURALIZATION/CITIZENSHIP FOR AN ADOPTED CHILD

In 1986, Senator Bill Bradley (D - N.J.) introduced an amendment which was signed into law in February 1987, which significantly changed the procedures for naturalizing your adopted child. There are now two ways in which families can obtain U.S. citizenship for their internationally adopted child. One way is to adhere to traditional naturalization procedure. A second way is to apply for a Certificate of Citizenship where the child is endowed with citizenship due to the status of his/her parents as U.S. citizens.

I. (Former Method): Naturalization of Adopted Child

In this procedure the child (or parent if child is too young) is interviewed and takes an oath of allegiance to the United States. This is the method used by most adults when they become citizens.

Requirements:

Application is usually made when adoption is finalized.
1. One parent only needs to be a U.S. citizen.
2. The child must be adopted before his/her 16th birthday.
3. If the child is under 14 years of age no fingerprints will be required.
4. The child must be naturalized before the age of 18.
5. It is not necessary for the child to know U.S. history or have knowledge of government. The child need not be able to read or speak English. The child will not be required to sign his own name.

Steps:

1. Request **Form N-402** and complete it, following the directions carefully.
2. Return the application with all the requested supporting documentation and photographs.
3. The family will receive a letter requesting them to appear before a naturalization examiner. One parent must appear in the company of the adopted child. A fee of $50 will be payable to the Immigration and Naturalization Service.
4. You will be notified to attend a final, swearing-in ceremony at a later date. This will be a court hearing.
5. A Certificate of Naturalization will be mailed to the family within several weeks.

II. (New Procedure): Applying for a Certificate of Citizenship for an Adopted Child

This method permits adopted children of U.S. citizens to become citizens through an administrative procedure.

Requirements:

1. Both parents **MUST** be U.S. citizens.
2. You must have a finalized adoption decree.
3. Child must be a permanent resident of the United States.
4. Child must have been adopted before the age of sixteen.

Steps:

1. Request **Form N-600** from the Immigration and Naturalization Service and complete it, following the directions carefully. Do not be alarmed if the form says "Not to be used by U.S. citizens." INS calculates it will take up to a year to use up the supply of old forms.
2. No interview or "swearing-in" ceremony is required. One parent will be asked to appear at the INS office to sign for and pick up the certificate. INS expects that in the future, the entire process can be accomplished by mail.

This method presently costs $35, and a check or money order must accompany the application.

Differences in the Former and New Procedures

1. Presently the new method involves only one visit to the INS office, with or without the child.
2. The new procedure is faster. The former procedure can cause as much as a year's delay due to a heavy court docket.
3. The new method is less expensive.
4. The new method does not necessitate an interview or hearing.
5. Method II is only possible if both parents are citizens.

There are advantages to both the old and new methods, depending on the circumstances or age of the child. Method I confers **citizenship by naturalization**. The child has all the rights of a person born in the U.S., but **cannot** be elected president.

Method II (the new method) is not a court proceeding; citizenship is conferred by right of parents' citizenship. This child has full rights of citizenship and could run for president if he/she wanted.

For the older child, method I has an additional advantage. The swearing in ceremony can be quite an emotional and dramatic event. This may be psychologically extremely important for the child to feel like a "real American." On occasion, schools have been able to arrange a field trip for the entire class to accompany the new citizen to the hearing as a lesson in government.

MEMENTOS OF THE DAY
THE CHILD RECEIVES HIS/HER CITIZENSHIP

In Michigan, the Department of Management and Budget will sell you a Michigan or U.S. flag and permit you to have it flown over the

State Capital on the day of your child's naturalization. You should send a check payable to the Department of Management and Budget for the cost of the flag and a request to "please fly my flag over the state capitol on ___(date)___." The flag will then be sent to you on the following day. Michigan flags are 3′ × 5′ and cost $25 for nylon and $18 for cotton. A cotton flag of the U.S. costs $13. If you are a Michigan resident and interested in purchasing a flag write:

State of Michigan (DMB)
Publications Office
7461 Crowner Drive
Lansing, MI 48913

You can get a letter from the president congratulating your child on citizenship by writing to:

White House Greetings Office
Old Executive Building, # 39
Washington, D.C. 20500

You can get the same kind of letter from your governor. In Michigan you can write:

Mr. Patrick Biehl
Governor's Communication Unit
P.O. Box 30013
Lansing, MI 48909

For other states, you can check wih the office of one of your Senators or Representatives for similar services.

All the forms you might need for your child's naturalization may be obtained by calling your **district office of the Immigration and Naturalization Service.** These are Listed in appendix D.

DEALING WITH OTHER PEOPLE — THEIR QUESTIONS ON ADOPTION, AS WELL AS RUDE, INSENSITIVE AND GENERALLY OBNOXIOUS BEHAVIORS

"Where's that baby from? He sure doesn't look like his mom and dad! Are there more where that one came from? Does he speak Spanish . . . (Korean) . . . ? Look at those big brown eyes . . ."

And on it goes . . . As an adoptive parent you learn very quickly that you are going to have to deal with such questions. How much information you want to share and with whom you want to share it is something each parent must decide for himself.

People, even well-intentioned individuals, can be extremely rude when it comes to discussing adoption. Total strangers will approach you and ask the most insensitive questions or make the stupidest comments. Most of the time they are just making conversation, yet it's easy to resent those comments.

If the child has big brown eyes, should you pretend he doesn't have them? Should you take offense at all such questions and behave defensively? This author has used some pat answers (not original, and I have heard others use them too) in reply to the more frequently asked questions.

Question: "Is that your REAL child?"
Answer: "Yes, she's real and I am her parent."

Question: "Where did she get those big eyes?"
Answer: "God gave them to her."

A few such retorts and the person asking the questions gets the idea you are not exactly thrilled with his/her questions.

As a parent, my concern has always been what the impact of such questions will be upon the child? I resent it when people ask these in front of a child who is too young to understand. All it serves to accomplish is to single out the child who then will feel "different" and uncomfortable. When the child is older and understands about adoption it doesn't bother me so much, but I still find it irksome and wonder why such people have the need to engage in this. The emphasis always seems to be on THE ADOPTION. As a parent, however, I feel I am far beyond that. I expect it should be taken for granted that I am the parent (**the real parent**) and that this is **my child.** It doesn't make a difference to me if he/she doesn't look like me or if he has those big brown eyes; why should it make a difference to someone else?

Similar feelings were expressed nicely by one adoptive mother in a recent "Dear Abby" letter. The letter is reproduced here, by permission of Universal Press Syndicate.*

---

*Taken from the "DEAR ABBY" column by Abigail Van Buren. Copyright 1987. Reprinted with permission of Universal Press Syndicate, all rights reserved.

Here's What Not To Say About Adopted Children, Whatever Their Heritage

Dear Abby: I'm the mother of four beautiful children, two of whom we adopted from India and Korea. With international adoptions becoming widespread, it would be a great service if you would print the following in the hope of educating some of the clods and well-meaning but thoughtless people out there:

•Please don't call my daughter Chinese. Not all Asians are Chinese, just as not all Caucasians are German. She is an American of Korean descent and proud of it.

•Please don't tell my children how lucky they are, as if they were poor little waifs in need of a handout. My husband and I are just as fortunate to have these wonderful children as they are to have us, and your attitude is patronizing. Anyway, a biological child owes his parents even more — he owes them his life!

•Please don't compliment them on how well they speak English. What else would they speak, having arrived in the United States as tiny infants? Besides, they'll laugh themselves sick at your expense in the car on the way home!

•Please give equal attention to our two biological children. All four will thank you — but don't spoil it by asking if they, too, are adopted. After all, it really is none of your business. And yes, Virginia, many people without fertility problems have chosen to adopt for other reasons.

•Please don't tell us about your cousin, neighbor or other acquaintances who have adopted. We're really tired of being stopped on the street to hear these tales, especially the ones that end with the woman becoming pregnant and having a baby of "her own" after all.

•Please spare us your speculations about what kind of villain their "real mother" (as the clods put it) must have been to give up such "cute" children. It takes a courageous and unselfish woman to give up a child she cannot care for, and it takes precious little character to get an abortion instead. Besides, you're very naive about the Third World culture and the conditions these women faced.

•Please let us go about our business. We're a family, not a sideshow, and we're often in a hurry. My children have feelings identical to yours, and it makes them very uncomfortable to stand listening while nosy strangers quiz us about their adoptions. Forgive me if I seem brusque on these occasions.

•Above all, M.Y.O.B. about my children's backgrounds: why they were given up, if their birth mothers were married, etc. I'm appalled by how often I have been asked such rude questions by friends, acquaintances and even strangers. This information is off limits to everyone outside our immediate family, and that means you, too, Aunt Mabel!

And to all you wonderful people who treat my children just like everyone else's, our sincere gratitude. You've got class with a capital "C"!

Sincerely, U.N. Mom

As I said previously, this is something each parent is going to have to come to terms with. Whether they want to accept these comments in stride and learn to live with them or react aggressive and defensively is an individual decision. After a while such questions stop bothering you, although this writer never ceases to be amazed at the lack of intelligence some people exhibit.

SOCIETY'S PERCEPTION OF ADOPTION

Our society does not have a very favorable image of adoption. As a parent, you may hear such comments as: "You can't love an adopted child as much as one of your own blood." Americans believe "blood will tell." Bad blood is similar to the "bad seed" idea (the time bomb waiting to explode). The thinking behind such a notion is that the original family environment must have been terrible. If not, why else would the child have been placed for adoption? Maybe the child's birthmother was a prostitute, the father a criminal . . . maybe both parents were drug addicts . . . what genetic surprises lie ahead for this well intentioned, but naive adoptive family?

Unless you have been touched by the adoption experience yourself it is difficult to understand that you can love an adopted child equally as your biologically produced offspring. You may believe this intellectually, but this is outside your realm of experience and difficult to feel in your heart.

Although society gives "lip service" to the value of adoption ("isn't that a nice thing to do") it does so with skepticism. Society is prejudiced against adoption and that prejudice is manifest in diverse ways.

Newspaper articles which emphasize "adoption" always imply that somehow the pathology told about in the story must in some way be connected with the fact that the child was "adopted." Would Mr. and Mrs. Steinberg of New York City have beaten to death their daughter if she were not adopted? Probably. Do birthparents also abuse children and sometimes kill them — of course they do, and to such a degree that it frequently isn't even deemed newsworthy. So why is there this need to emphasize that this was an "adopted" child, if not to imply something negative about adoption or that the adoptive system is bad (although in this case the attorney-murderer bypassed the system).

What about notorious criminals like David Berkowitz, the "Son of Sam" killer, or Kenneth Bianci, the "Hillside Strangler." By mentioning the fact that these individuals were adopted, was not the newspaper implying that some other adopted child could become a killer? Perhaps only given the right circumstances, the "bad blood" would tell.

The phrase "adopted-child syndrome," coined by psychologists David Kirschner and Arthur Sorosky supports the notion that the rage felt by such killers is connected to feelings of rejection and abandonment felt by adopted children.[2] In the right circumstances that rage bursts forth and you have a "hillside strangler." Of course the validity of the thinking behind the "adopted child syndrome" is dubious and there has been little scientific evidence to support such a notion. Francine Klagsbrun has noted that the phrase itself may have been nothing more than a device to beef up a weak criminal defense.[3] Unfortunately, it sounds credible and the result is merely to further stigmatize adopted children.

The way adoption is portrayed in the media is only one manifestation of our prejudice against adoption. How we treat girls thinking of releasing their child for adoptive placement is another. Instead of encouraging them to give "the gift of life," society often interrogates them, makes them feel ashamed and guilty about what they are contemplating.

As a director of an adoption agency I have seen this happen again and' again and seen thoughtless people (including so called "professionals"), behave badly towards such women.

Recently at Children's Hope we had a judge who was so verbally abusive to a girl considering adoption that he forced her to near hysteria. He did this merely because she was going to release her child for adoptive placement.

"Are you sure you want to do this?" he demanded repeatedly, unable to accept that this could truly be the woman's wish. "Have you given this careful consideration? Are you absolutely sure this is what you want to do?"

He posed these questions to the woman so many times and with such exasperation that she finally broke down in the courtroom, unable to speak due to her tears. Yet, she remained steadfast in her resolve to do what she felt to be best for her child despite this judge's lack of sympathy or understanding.

In another case, Children's Hope was prevented from placing an infant with an adoptive family for three months. The probate judge

---

2. Pamela V. Grabe, ed., *Adoption Resources for Mental Health Professionals* (Mercer, PA: The Children's Aid Society in Mercer County, 1986), p. 40.

3. Francine Klagsbrun, "Debunking the 'Adopted Child Syndrome Myth," *OURS: The Magazine of Adoptive Families,* July/August 1987, p. 20.

insisted that instead of placing the baby with the adoptive family, we place the baby in "preadoptive placement" while we wait to see if the putative, biological father would appear to accept his paternal responsibility. This decision was made after accepting a valid release of maternal rights from the mother, who now, by law, had no legal interest in the child. The judge decided to adopt a "wait and see" attitude. Of all the people involved, the judge gave chief concern to the biological father, who had demonstrated no interest in the child whatsoever. He put the interests of the putative father ahead of those of the birthmother, the adoptive family, and the child himself.

Compare this treatment to that given to persons who decide to have an abortion or to raise their child themselves? Court cases have held that even if the father comes forth and requests to raise the child and assume all financial responsibility, he cannot interfere with the mother's "right" to choose an abortion. Why should the father have so much say in matters of adoption (allowing him three months to come forward), but so little say in the decision to terminate a pregnancy? Why would the woman have a "right" to choose an abortion, (overriding the father's objections), but not have the same right if she wants to place her child with an adoptive family (even if the father refuses to acknowledge the child's existence)?

In most states, a woman can decide to have an abortion without her parents' consent or even knowledge. For example, if my daughter wanted to undergo an abortion, it is not required that I be informed; but, if she wanted to have her ears pierced, I would have to consent to what amounted to "surgery." In fact, if my daughter wanted to ride the school bus to a class outing I would first have, not only to be informed, but also to give my permission or she wouldn't be allowed to participate in the outing.

If a new mother decides not to undergo an abortion, our society encourages her to keep her child herself, even if she is too young and obviously not ready to be a parent. She is sent to an "alternative education" classroom to teach her parenting skills, and she is eligible for welfare to take care of her financial needs. We do this because, as a society, we have a commitment to families; families are seen as good things.

But, somehow, adoptive families are perceived differently. We don't have the same commitment to adoptive families and the social system we have created has evolved to make adoptive placements difficult. Children languish in foster care for years while prospective adoptive parents wait years in anticipation of adopting those children.

The image society has of adoptive families is different than the conception of what a "real family" should be like. A "real family" is supposed to be composed of two parents, a full-time mother and 2.5 biologically produced children. The conception we Americans have of the family is largely a fantasy based more on television portrayals (circa the 1960's) of domestic life than in terms of today's reality.

But, as we said earlier; you have yourself to be involved with an adoptive relationship to realize that adoptive families are "real" families and that an adopted child can be loved and love in return, as much as any biological child.

In an effort to counteract prejudice against adoption and to foster a more positive image, the **National Committee For Adoption** has been providing inserts in leading publications. These were developed by **Tim Love Advertising** in New York City and have been successful in promoting a more positive image of the adopted child.

DEALING WITH RACIAL PREJUDICE

Racial prejudice when directed towards your child is very disturbing. As a parent who loves his or her child nothing can be more painful than to see him/her ostracized for something over which he has no control.

Racism in our society is pervasive and subtle. Even many of our prospective parents reveal it in one form or another. At Children's Hope, we constantly get questioned, "How dark will the skin be?" We have had prospective parents reject referrals from some countries because they felt the child would be darker than if he/she came from another country. There is a point of demarcation in the minds of these people as to what is acceptable.

The forms of prejudice an adopted parent may encounter from others will be varied. People might make disparaging comments. They might turn their faces away or refuse to sit next to the child. It could be subtle or hidden, such as talking about the child when you are not even present.

Racial prejudice with older children becomes more apparent during school years. Children may hear direct racial slurs, ethnic jokes or disparaging comments about their features or skin color. They may find it difficult to date or may be excluded from participating in school clubs. Parents need to prepare children for such possibilities and impart a sense of pride in the child's heritage. Making a **"life-book,"** may be one way of accomplishing this, using pictures from both countries and illustrating the child's "uniqueness." This can convey the sense of unconditional positive regard with which the parents hold the child.

It goes without saying that parents themselves should use positive language when talking about the birth-country in the presence of the child. They should avoid talking about the people as impoverished, illiterate or uneducated. They should not make racial stereotypes or ethnic jokes serving to portray persons of the child's birth-country (or any other racial group) in a negative manner. Rather, parents should discuss plans to some day again visit the country when the child is older so the child can see what a wonderful place he/she came from. They should mention all the attributes of the foreign culture and stress the positive.

A child needs to have a satisfactory explanation presented as to who they are and how they came to be part of the family. It is essential in developing a sense of self-esteem and pride that the child develop a positive image of him/herself as a unique and integral part of the family unit. The child's self-image will be determined more than anything else from the manner in which he/she is treated by the parents. Ideally, that will be with love and unconditional acceptance.

ETHNICITY, HERITAGE AND SOCIETAL PRESSURE

As a society we have moved quite far from the "melting pot" philosophy which expected us all to blend together to a homogeneous unit. Since the civil rights movement of the 1960's there has been an ever greater emphasis in establishing individual as well as group identity and pride. Such expressions as "Black power," "Hispanic pride," "Indian self-determination" put the emphasis on racial and cultural differences.

This trend is endorsed officially by affirmative action programs designed to create a proportionate representation by race in business and education, and minority study programs in colleges and universities.[4] In matters of adoption, such trends have manifested themselves in the position that transracial placements should be avoided and a child should be placed only in an adoptive home where parents are of the same ethnic background. This is currently the law with respect to Native American children who can be placed in adoptive homes only with other Native Americans families, unless an exception is granted by the Tribal Council.

Parents who have adopted internationally face somewhat of a problem in trying to understand these issues. Most cling tenaciously to the

---

4. John E. Williams and J. Kenneth Morland, *Race, Color and the Young Child.* (The University of N. Carolina Press, 1976) pp. 30-31.

"melting pot" theory which they learned and believed as children. On a personal, family level, they have seen that the theory can work and work very well. These parents are appalled at the suggestion that there is anything wrong in the placement of **their** child. When they hear that the child would have been better left in his/her country of origin or should be placed with another family (usually of the same ethnic background), they are angered; to them, such arguments are ridiculous.

Yet, trends in adoption have been proceeding in this direction for some time. Within the child welfare system, restricted placements making "racial matching" the principal criteria were becoming the norm. Only those who adopted internationally, expending large sums of money, were exempt from these policies because they had managed to bypass the state welfare bureaucracy.

In 1986 the Massachusetts Urban League introduced a bill to the State Legislature restricting the placement of Black and Hispanic children with family members or families of the same ethnic and racial background. In 1987 they tried to extend this to include Asian children as well.[5]

The Urban League and others have advocated a position that transracial adoptions are detrimental to the children involved and that by being placed with a family of a different racial background the child will suffer psychological damage. Although this position has many adherents, it does not seem to be supported by the evidence. Research indicates that the things which will cause harm are not those which arise out of differences in race between parent and child. What appears to be crucial is the degree of support within the family environment, as well as the sensitivity the family has towards the child's uniqueness, including his racial background. Factors such as acquisition of English, early academic success and the development of positive social contacts are also important.[6]

A significant factor in the development of subsequent maladjustment does not seem even related to race, but rather, to the length of time the child had remained in his preadoptive environment.[7]

In 1986 a U.S. District Court in Michigan signed a consent decree amending the existing practices of the Michigan Department of Social Services. The Department had been using "racial matching" as the principal criterion, to the extent that they removed a Black child from a very

---

5. "Massachusetts Urban League, Inc. to Submit Bill to Limit Child Placements to 'Matching' Race Parents," *Joint Council Bulletin,* 5, No. 5 (1986), 3.

6. Mary Ellen Harris-Warren, "A Case Study of Foreign Street Children's Adjustment and Assimilation into the American Culture," Diss Univ. of Connecticut, 1984, pp. 455-471.

7. Silverman, pp. 226-227.

successful foster care placement with a White family and placed the child with a Black family. Their sole reason for doing this was that the second family was Black. Although the child had been making a good adjustment and was with a loving family for a considerable length of time, these things were not considered crucial. A lawsuit filed by the American Civil Liberties Union on behalf of the **Committee to End Racism in Michigan's Child Care System** sought to challenge the existing policy.

The lawsuit resulted in the amendment of these regulations. The court decided that although a racially-matched placement would be preferable, race would be only one criterion considered. More importantly, the placement should be made " . . . according to the best interests of the child." With respect to children of mixed heritage (Black/White), the court said these children shall no longer be regarded as Black and placed only in Black homes, but " . . . a child of mixed race parentage shall be placed with a family whose background is similar . . . or with a family . . . that possesses the interest, capacity, and disposition to appreciate and educate the child about the child's racial, ethnic, and cultural heritage and background."[8]

For the families of internationally adopted children, arguments over racial restrictions are interesting but pedantic. Such parents have experienced the joy the child has brought in their lives, and whether the child has almond shaped eyes or a darker complexion is irrelevant. These families are committed to such children to the fullest extent possible. They provide their total resources (materially, spiritually, and educationally) to see the child reach his/her full potential.

As a director of a program for international adoption I have placed many such children. In almost every case the parents become tearful and indicate:

"This is the most beautiful baby in the whole world!"

I have seen these children prosper and thrive with their new families and there is not the slightest doubt in my mind as to the inherent worthiness of such placements.

Nevertheless, the baby does not stay a baby forever. These children and their families might very well face, during adolescence, problems regarding issues of adoption and transracial placement. This will be a stressful time in their lives and parents should be prepared for that possibility. They likely will have some very important issues to deal with later.

---

8. Susan Gabriel, "Michigan Committee Wins Discrimination Case," *The Children's Voice*, March 1986, pp. 1-2.

CHAPTER 12

HEALTH CONSIDERATIONS
OF FOREIGN-BORN CHILDREN

BEFORE OBTAINING your child's visa so that your child may emigrate, you are given a list of approved doctors in the foreign country. You are required to take the child for a medical examination to one of these physicians. The doctor will present you with a sealed envelope to deliver to the embassy indicating the result of the examination. There are certain conditions which will prevent a child's entrance into the United States, such as untreated tuberculosis, AIDS, and other communicable diseases.

If the child was presented a visa by the U.S. Embassy, the results of the examination were negative and he/she will be allowed to enter the U.S. However, that should not be interpreted that the child is free from medical problems or that he or she should not be re-examined once the family returns home. Medical examinations overseas for adoption may be quite superficial. In the first days or weeks home the adoptive parent should take the child to a physician.

Although most children who come to the United States via adoption are in reasonably good condition[1], there is always the possibility the child may be suffering from some unapparent or undiagnosed medical condition. There may be little, if any, medical history. No information on the parents or biological family may exist. The child's development may be delayed due to neglect or institutionalization, and he may be smaller than his North American counterpart. His age may only be an estimate. For these reasons, comparison with medical statistics of North American children might not be appropriate. Each child should be examined carefully and critically to ascertain any unknown medical problem.

---

1. Anne Welsbacher, "Assessing Your Child's Health Needs," *OURS: The Magazine of Adoptive Families*, July/August 1987, p. 12.

Children from overseas surrendered for adoption might suffer from malnutrition. They may appear unusually small for their age, listless, perhaps with a protruding abdomen. This condition is fairly obvious. More likely, however, the child will simply be under-nourished. This is not as easy to identify. The child will seem smaller than "average" and somewhat "delayed." He/she may have a lowered resistance to infection, be anemic, and recover more slowly from illness due to nutritional deficiency.

A 1985 study of adopted children screened 360 Korean adoptees placed by Associated Catholic Charities of Baltimore. The study found it wise to screen adopted children for certain health conditions. Although adopted children did not appear to have infectious conditions different from native born children, they ran greater risks of having some preexisting health problem if they came from a region where those problems are endemic.[2]

A 1984 study by Jerri Ann Jenista, M.D. and Daniel Chapman, M.D. of 128 adopted children in Michigan concluded that the majority of the children were perfectly healthy. The major problems found were deficient immunizations (37%), intestinal parasites (29%), emotional or behavioral problems (22%), skin diseases (16%), estimated age (12%), scabies and/or lice (10%). Almost half the children had an acute infectious disease (including upper respiratory tract infection, ear infections, measles, chickenpox or mumps) within the first month after arrival in the United States. In addition, "surgical procedures ranging from circumcision to cleft lip palate repair" were required for 19% of the children. Other less common medical conditions include "developmental delay, lactose intolerance, vision and hearing deficits and chronic hepatitis B carrier status" were also identified.[3]

The following is a brief description of selected health problems which might be encountered by adoptive parents and for which they might want to have their child examined.

VIRAL INFECTIONS

Hepatitis B

Hepatitis B virus is one of the causes of hepatitis, a disease of the liver. There are several forms of hepatitis and it is important that

---

2. W. Robert Lange, M.D., M.P.H. and Ellen Warnock-Eckhart, M.S.W., "Selected Infectious Disease Risks in International Adoptees," *The Pediatric Infectious Disease Journal*, 6, No. 5 (1987), 447.

3. Jerri Ann Jenista, M.D., and Daniel Chapman, M.D., "Medical Problems of Foreign-Born Adopted Children," *American Journal of Diseases of Children*, 141 (1987), pp. 298-302.

Hepatitis B not be confused with Hepatitis A (previously called "infectious hepatitis") or other forms of hepatitis.

Hepatitis B is a disease found more commonly in certain parts of the world than others. In Asia an estimated "5-15% of the population are carriers of the virus compared to less than 1% in the United States. . . . "[4] Consequently, people adopting from this region of the world must understand the possibility that their adopted child might have been exposed to this virus. A person contracts this disease by direct exposure to the virus in the blood stream. This can happen to a newborn during delivery or from a blood transfusion. The virus can also be transmitted during intimate sexual contact. Symptoms of the infection may include jaundice, nausea, vomiting or fever. Most children and some adults will not exhibit any symptoms. If the person manufactures antibodies sufficient to overcome the infection he or she becomes immune to the virus and is not contagious to others.

Depending on the age at which a person acquires Hepatitis B, he or she may not be able to produce sufficient antibodies to overcome the infection. The virus remains in the person's blood stream and liver although the individual does not exhibit any symptoms of the disease. This is referred to as a **Hepatitis B carrier,** a condition in which the individual is contagious, **but only by blood or other intimate** contact.

The carrier state is important to identify for families who have adopted children from any developing nation including Latin America. About 5% of Korean or East Indian children and 1-2% of Latin American children will be carriers. Up to 30% of all children will have antibodies but no active virus, indicating **past exposure** and **immunity** to hepatitis B. The risk of other family members getting the disease may be as high as 30-60% if the adopted child is a carrier. Evidence shows that persons in the carrier state are more likely to develop other liver diseases, such as cirrhosis of the liver or cancer of the liver. These diseases take a long time to manifest themselves, perhaps 30 to 40 years, but the risks of getting them are greater if an individual is a carrier (there is no increased risk if the person has been **exposed** but is **not** a carrier). Consequently, parents should have the carrier child regularly monitored by a physician.

If the family has a carrier child, **the family members should all receive Hepatitis B vaccine.** This is a very safe and effective vaccine to prevent transmission of the disease. Parents will then need to be concerned about the child. As years pass, they will need to have the child regularly examined to detect signs of further liver damage. Parents will

---

4. Charles J. Zelnick, M.D., "Hepatitis B and Overseas Adoption," *Adoption Today,* 6, No. 1 (1986), 25.

also need to monitor the child's activities to **determine who should be informed about the child's carrier status**. Vaccines are not recommended for school contacts and the risk of infection is extremely low.[5] Since transmission of the infection requires direct contact with the blood stream or other bodily fluids it might not be necessary to inform all those in everyday contact with the child. Of course, if there are those who come in prolonged contact with the child such as live-in child care workers or day care workers they should be told and vaccinated. Even if it is a situation more casual, but where children might fight, bite, scratch or put fingers in each other's mouth, parents should be advised. This is controversial. If the child is of school-age, there is probably no need to inform **anyone** as the child is old enough to report significant exposures, i.e., a bleeding cut, a bite breaking the skin, etc. In the preschool child, it might be better for the parent to be selective about choosing playmates, rather than inform everyone (Sunday school, next door neighbors etc.) with which the child comes in contact. Casual transmission is extremely rare and telling anyone outside the family risks labelling the child as a pariah.

Yet, a responsible parent realizes that some people have a right to this information. If the child was spending the night at the home of a friend, undoubtedly the friend's parents would want to know of the carrier status of their guest and take appropriate hygienic precautions. But, if the child is old enough to spend the night, he is also old enough to practice good hygiene by himself. In that case, other children's parents might need to be informed **only** if an accident occurs. Again, returning to the idea of being "labeled," people tend to panic concerning infectious disease, no matter how remote the possibility of transmission.

Although courts have ruled that schools cannot exclude or segregate such children, news reports in the popular media continually remind us of how callous men can be to one another. Parents must weigh carefully who it would be wise to inform or not to inform about such a sensitive issue. The stigma and negative attention focused upon a child as a result of such a revelation could be far more damaging than the viral infection itself.

As Charles J. Zelnick, M.D. reported in an article on Hepatitis B in the Spring 1986 issue of *Adoption Today* (Adoption Services of WACAP):

> . . . "it is important to keep the problem of Hepatitis B in perspective. Although this is an infectious disease with a very interesting and complex transmission pattern and with possible long-term adverse effects,

---

5. Ronald C. Hershow, M.D., Stephen C. Hadler, M.D., and Mark A. Kane, M.D., "Adoption of Children from Countries with Endemic Hepatitis B: Transmission Risks and Medical Issues," *The Pediatric Infectious Disease Journal*, 6, No. 5 (1987), 431-437.

it is important to remember that in the Orient it is an extremely common, everyday illness. None of our adopted children come with a guarantee that they will be 100% healthy. It is sometimes helpful to remember that Hepatitis B infection may be preferable to other types of parasitic or bacterial infections or to birth defects. My attitude is that the primary job of parents is to teach their children to survive and adapt to what Hamlet calls the 'slings and arrows of outrageous fortune.' Thus, learning to overcome a congenital infection can and should be viewed as a learning experience. As Dr. Jenista, Professor of Pediatrics at the University of Michigan states, 'This is not a perfect world; we cannot protect our children 100% from every threat, whether it is infection or accident or violence. Maintaining a calm attitude and adopting a practical plan that allows a normal lifestyle seems to me the most realistic solution' And as one mother of a Hepatitis B carrier states, she remembers her doctor helping her put her situation in perspective when he said, 'This is a small price to pay for a beautiful family.' "[6]

AIDS (Acquired Immunodeficiency Syndrome)

Although there has been a lot of information concerning AIDS during the last two years, little has been written concerning children placed for adoption with this condition. Since May of 1987, regularly, there have appeared messages on the telecommunication network (electronic bulletin board) of the National Adoption Exchange regarding such children.

Message 689-9
Subj: RESEARCH ON ADOPTING CHILDREN WITH AIDS
ACCORDING TO THE JUNE 1, 1987 STATISTICS RELEASED BY THE CENTERS FOR DISEASE CONTROL IN ATLANTA, GA. THERE ARE 504 CHILDREN UNDER THE AGE OF 13 WITH AIDS NATIONWIDE. ABOUT ONE-THIRD OF THE CHILDREN BORN TO AIDS-INFECTED MOTHERS WILL GO ON TO DEVELOP AIDS, AND BETWEEN 25 AND 35 PERCENT OF THESE CHILDREN WILL NEED SUBSTITUTE CARE BECAUSE THEIR MOTHERS ARE EITHER DRUG ADDICTS OR TOO SICK TO CARE FOR THE CHILDREN. SOME ADOLESCENTS WITH AIDS MAY ALSO NEED SUBSTITUTE CARE. AS THE NUMBERS OF THESE CASES INCREASE, SO WILL THE NEED FOR CLEAR POLICIES ON ADOPTION AND FOSTER CARE . . . [7]

---

6. Zelnick, p. 27.

7. Adoption Exchange Announcement, June 1, 1987.

Of the Adoption Exchange messages having to do with AIDS, most reflect the difficulty of placing a child with AIDS or the special services needed once a family is found. In these situations, the family knows in advance the child has AIDS and willingly accepts the child.

Another possibility is that a family will adopt a child internationally, believing the child is healthy, and later discover the child has AIDS. The possibility of this happening at the time of this writing is extremely small, but the possibility does exist. It is not so much a matter of whether or not such an event can occur, "but when will it happen?"[8]

AIDS is caused by a virus called HTLV-III or LAV or HIV which attacks the person's immune system, leaving him susceptible to a host of infections, any of which can be fatal to the patient. AIDS has a long incubation period which can be from 6 months to more than 5 years. Not all persons develop the full-blown syndrome, however. Some, though they have persistent infections with few if any symptoms, develop what Dr. James Curran of the CDC task force on AIDS describes as a "peaceful coexistence with the virus . . . but they have persistent infection and are probably persistently infectious to others."[9] Others develop the symptoms of fatigue, weight loss, diarrhea, swollen glands or night sweats, without actually developing the fatal illness. This condition is referred to medically as **ARC** or **AIDS-Related-Complex** and, although some individuals seem to live with this status only, most ARC patients go on to develop the full-blown AIDS.

The probability of adopting a foreign-born child with AIDS is extremely small. This chance can be made even smaller if certain precautions are taken. If the child you are adopting is from a country with a high probability of an individual having AIDS, the medical background of the birth-family should be studied carefully to determine if there is a history of intravenous drug use, prostitution or homosexuality. A blood test called an HTLV-III or HIV antibody test can be done to determine whether or not the child has been exposed to the AIDS virus. This test should cost about $50, a small price to pay for peace of mind. The result could be provided when the referral is made and the medical report and photographs are presented to the potential adoptive parent. However, the test is not a guarantee that the child will develop AIDS, and **a negative finding does not insure that the child will not develop AIDS at**

8. Jerri Ann Jenista, M.D. "AIDS and Internationally Adopted Children," *OURS: The Magazine of Adoptive Families*, July/August 1987, p. 14.

9. Claudia Wallis, as Reported by Patricia Delaney, Joyce Leviton and Melissa Ludtke, "AIDS: A growing Threat," *TIME*, 12 August 1986, p. 42.

some later date. The virus could be incubating and not be diagnosable in the child until much later. Also, a positive test could be a "false positive," which is more likely overseas where the tests might not be performed as carefully as in U.S. research laboratories.

Although AIDS is not currently one of the medical problems adoptive parents can expect, the future is unknown. The U.S. Public Health Service predicts that approximately 270,000 cases of AIDS will have occurred in the United States by 1991, making AIDS a medical problem of extraordinary proportions.[10]

AIDS is no longer an affliction of certain high risk population only, but of the general population as well. We undoubtedly will hear more and more about AIDS in the future. At Children's Hope we sometimes receive requests by adoptive parents to have their referral screened for AIDS. We try and explain how unlikely it would be to get a baby with AIDS and that you can't get a reliable diagnosis unless the baby has several different tests repeated over a six month period of time.

In July of 1987 the regulations were changed with respect to overseas medical examinations and AIDS. All children over fifteen will be required to have a blood test for the virus. However, that will not be necessary for infants unless there is a feeling by the physician that the child might have AIDS. You cannot tell whether a baby has AIDS by looking at the baby. It is not yet clear how often physicians will recommend such tests for orphan visas.

TUBERCULOSIS

Tuberculosis is a disease caused by a very slow-growing bacterium, mycobacterium tuberculosis, which is particularly common in underdeveloped, poorer countries, although more than 20,00 new cases are reported each year in the U.S. Tuberculosis is usually acquired in one of two ways, 1) breathing in the infected respiratory secretions of an individual with tuberculosis of the lungs or 2) drinking the milk of an infected cow (bovine type tuberculosis which affects both cows and men). Tuberculosis is a chronic inflammation and the individual may remain for years without any sign of damage due to the body's natural defensive ability. However, the possibility is always there, that under the right circumstances (another infection, poor nutrition or bad health conditions),

---

10. Jonathan M. Mann, "The global AIDS situation," *World Health: The Magazine of the World Health Organization*, June 1987, p. 6.

the infection will overcome the host victim. Tuberculosis used to be the greatest killer of mankind and was known by such names as "Consumption" and the "Great White Plague." It is still a very serious health problem in terms of "world health," with mortality reaching nearly three million annually. If an adopted child comes from an underdeveloped nation it is a good idea to have him/her thoroughly examined for signs of this disease. Usually a skin test and/or a chest x-ray is sufficient.

VENEREAL DISEASE

Venereal disease in a pregnant woman may be transferred to her offspring and leave the child severely impaired. Herpes and many other venereal infections (for example, non-gonoccal urethritis, chancroid, lymphogranuloma venereum and granuloma inguinale) can all seriously affect a newborn baby. However, these diseases are quite rare and the child is usually obviously ill.

A more common condition is gonorrhea. A child born from a woman with gonorrhea can develop severe inflammation of the eyes (gonococcal conjunctivitis) which left untreated may leave the child permanently blind. This is not a subtle disease and would not be missed even in the worst of child care situations.

Syphilis may be passed from an infected pregnant woman to her child. If the syphilis is transferred early in the pregnancy it usually results in a miscarriage or stillbirth. However, if the disease is transferred later in the pregnancy, the child may display the symptoms of congenital syphilis as he grows older. Since there are frequently no signs of syphilis in the first months of life, it is important the infant be tested since treatment with antibiotics will completely cure the disease. If the child is left untreated, however, he/she may develop many of the effects of thirdstage syphilis much later in life. Syphilis tests are frequently performed by orphanages and are often requested in the visa examination. You should check these records carefully as you may be able to avoid this test.

LEPROSY (Hansen's Disease)

Leprosy is an infection caused by the lepra baccillus (Mycobacterium laprae). Although the disease still affects approximately 11 million persons it is confined to regions of the world where the climate is hot and moist, such as the west coast of India or equatorial regions of Asia, Africa and South America. A 1983 issue of *Newsweek* Magazine reported that for that year, 232 new cases of leprosy had been diagnosed in the United States. These were mostly from new immigrants, bringing the national total to more than 4,000 cases.[11] It is **extremely unlikely** that a child brought to the United States for adoption would have leprosy. The incubation period is extremely long (years) and diagnosis is rarely made even by adolescence.

PARASITES

Other conditions are less serious but can be troublesome including infestation by parasites and diseases resulting from poor nutrition or inadequate hygiene.

All children adopted from developing countries should **be screened for parasites**. It is likely a child infected will show no outward signs. A stool sample should be sent to a laboratory for an "ova and parasite" examination. One negative result should not be considered definitive since some parasites may not be shedding ova (eggs) into the stool at that time. Periodic testing should continue for at least six months after arrival, with a minimum of three tests giving negative results.

Protozoa (Entamoeba hystolytica) cause amoebic dysentery which is an acute inflammation of the digestive tract and a very serious medical condition. The child will appear listless and have severe diarrhea which will also have mucus, pus and blood in the stools.

Worm infestation, can also cause serious health problems. These may include (1) **hookworms** (Ankylostoma duodenale), which bore through the bare feet of children and are carried by the blood to the lungs. These worms climb the trachea, descend the esophagus, go through the stomach and lodge in the intestine. Here they remain, sucking the child's blood and causing weakness and anemia. (2) **roundworms** (Ascaris lumbricoides), which enter the intestines when children swallow the eggs on uncooked vegetables, grow to about the size of an earthworm. They too live in the intestine and cause debilitation and weakness. (3) **Pinworms** and **threadworms** (Enterobius vermicularis) are small worms which resemble white threads. They cause severe itching around the anus and may cause children to develop nervous disturbances or even to go into convulsions.

---

11. Jean Seligmann with Gary Esolen, Richard Sandza and Deborah Witherspoon, "The Unmentionable Disease," *Newsweek*, 31 January 1983, p. 67.

Other roundworms which can affect the health of both children and adults include the **muscleworm** (Trichinella spiralis) which can cause trichinosis if an individual eats improperly prepared pork, and filaria, which causes an obstruction of the lymph system known in tropical lands as Elephantiasis.

Another type of worm is the **tapeworm** (cestodes) which gets its name from its unusual shape which resemble a piece of tape. Still other worms are known as flukes (unsegmented worms) which are prevalent in certain parts of the world and cause a disease known as schistosomiasis.

Chronic infections still plague vast segments of the population in many nations of the world. At present time there are more than 200 million malaria cases in the world, 260 million hookworm cases, 650 million people with ascarids (a roundworm), and 5 million cases of leprosy, of which 3 million are in Asia. Asia has 335 million people who habor the parasitic ascarid. Each of these Asians will harbor between six and nine adult ascarids. The worms thus carried by these 335 million Asians will consume as much food each day as a population of more than 40,000 people.[12]

WHAT AN ADOPTIVE PARENT SHOULD KNOW ABOUT INTERNAL PARASITES

From a practical point of view, the adoptive parent needs to be aware of the following:

(1) There is no predicting from symptoms which parasite a child might have. You need to have a proper diagnostic test performed in a laboratory.

(2) Most internal parasites are not contagious to the rest of the family. The cantagious ones such as amoeba and giardia are also common in the United States.

(3) A low level infestation may never be detected by a stool examination. You should not be unduly alarmed if you see your child pass a worm even after you have been assured your child was free from internal parasites.

(4) Treatment is usually easy but may be expensive.

(5) Good family hygiene, such as **handwashing** is extremely important.

---

12. Lawrence W. Green and C.L. Anderson, *Community Health*, 5th ed. (St. Louis: Times Mirror/ Mosby, 1986) p. 63.

EXTERNAL PARASITES

There are also external parasites, such as the arthropods, which can affect children. One animal, Acarus scabiei, a small mite, causes a condition known as "scabies." The female burrows into the child's skin to deposit her eggs. This causes intense irritation and itching two to six weeks after exposure.

The **head louse** (Pediculus capitis) lives in the hair and causes irritation of the scalp. More serious is the **body louse** (Pediculus corporis) which lives on the skin and breeds in the clothing. This louse may carry disease such as typhus fever and is more irritating than the head louse. Scabies and lice are both easily treated with one or two applications of drugs such as Kwell or Nix. They can be annoying to get rid of but will not harm the child in the long run.

FUNGAL INFECTIONS

Fungal infections favor high humidity, warmth and a free oxygen supply. For this reason they are more common in the tropics and can cause serious health problems. Fungi may cause superficial or systemic infections in man and be more resistant than bacteria to drying or treatment with antibiotics. Fungus disease depends not only on the strength of the organism, but the diminished resistance **(opportunistic fungus infection)** of the host. Therefore, it is particularly apparent in neglected children who have been "wasting" as a result of poor nutrition and care. Since moisture favors the growth of fungus, common sites of infection are the mouth (moniliasis, known as **thrush**) vagina, and urinary tract. Fungus infections may also occur on the skin (dermatomycoses — known as **ringworm**). Some of these are common in the United States and easily recognized by any pediatrician.

A nutritional disease for which adopted children might be examined is **Rickets**. This disease of young children is the result of insufficient calcium or vitamin D absorption. Calcium comes from the child's food supply and is deposited in bones. If the child lacks vitamin D which enables the body to absorb calcium or does not get enough sunlight (ultraviolet light stimulates the production of vitamin D) rickets may result. Children with this disease will have soft bones which may bend or result in deformity. Nutritional rickets is extremely easily cured with a well-balanced American diet. A child who is not growing well after several months on a good diet is a candidate for an x-ray of a leg or an arm to diagnose rickets.

LACTOSE INTOLERANCE

This is a gastrointestinal condition where a child is unable to properly digest cow's milk or cow's milk formulas due to a lack of the enzyme needed for digesting lactose. There are two forms of lactose intolerance. The hereditary form is common in Orientals and all dark-skinned peoples and may be only a partial deficiency of the enzyme. The acquired form is frequent after diarrhea or during malnutrition. It is gradually reversible. Symptoms include cramps, gas, bloating, diarrhea and nausea. If a child has this condition, soybean formulas can be substituted. For older children, the missing enzyme, lactase, may be added to dairy products. It is sold in drug stores as a powder of liquid called Lactaid.

WHAT YOU SHOULD ADVISE YOUR DOCTOR — WHERE YOU CAN GO FOR HELP

Physicians who do not come into contact with some of the more exotic conditions of adopted children may incorrectly diagnose the disease. They might see an undernourished child and immediately hospitalize him/her because they are not certain just what to do. Parents should tell the doctors as much as they can about where the child comes from and the known medical and genetic history. Local parent groups may be able to advise parents as to physicians who are qualified to diagnose and treat problems associated with foreign-born adopted children. Don't forget your child needs all the usual well child care given to U.S. born children. The most common mistake is to focus on the exotic disease and miss the immunizations or the hearing problems or the allergies.

For those parents who are especially concerned about a particular health problem, there is a clinic especially geared to treating children adopted from overseas. The **International Adoption Clinic** is part of the University of Minnesota Hospital. The clinic was founded by Dr. and Mrs. Dana Johnson after they adopted a child from India and learned how difficult it was to receive impartial and objective medical treatment for their adopted child. Currently the staff of the clinic encourages telephone calls from adoptive parents concerned about their child's health status. Telephone numbers for the clinic are:

(612) 626-2928   (612) 626-6777
(612) 626-2971   (612) 624-6907

Parents who would like to write to the clinic directly should address their correspondence to:

International Adoption Clinic
Box 211, University Hospital
Harvard at East River Road
Minneapolis, MN 55455

In Michigan, the clinic will likely refer parents to Dr. Jerri Jenista at the University of Michigan Medical Center. Parents wanting to contact Dr. Jenista directly, should call (313) 763-2440. Her mailing address is:

Jerri Ann Jenista, M.D.
Pediatric Infectious Diseases
F7828/0244, C.S. Mott Children's Hospital
University of Michigan Medical Center
1500 East Medical Center Drive
Ann Arbor, MI 48109-0244

CHAPTER 13

SOME FINAL THOUGHTS

WE CONTINUE to receive letters from parents who have successfully completed the international adoption process. Here is what some of our clients have said:

"Adoption is not for families who are easily discouraged. There were disappointments and challenges too in the search for our son. In many ways the wait for John was similar to the wait during a pregnancy. Not knowing what he would look like, when he would come, loving him in our hearts even before we held him in our arms. . . . "

"We love our new son so very much. All the forms, paperwork and waiting in the adoption process were worth it. He is such a blessing each and every day. . . . "

"Adoption has been the hardest thing that we as a family have had to deal with. . . . We didn't mind the paperwork—it kept us busy as we waited. The hardest part was the waiting for the phone to ring. I've always read you'll get the call when you least expect it—and that certainly is true! . . . Now, when I look at our baby, I think, thank God for him. He's such a wonder and miracle to us. . . . Believe me, all that paperwork, all the minor details, all of the wondering and waiting were worth it, when you finally have that special baby or child in your arms. . . . "

"It's almost hard to believe he's finally here! All the anxious moments and frustrations were worth it. . . . "

The above comments make up a very small sample of remarks from the many letters we receive. All these parents remember the difficulties, the reams of paperwork, and, most of all, the seemingly endless wait. But, for almost everyone, the wait results in a happy ending. And with the arrival of the newest family member, the frustrations seem to fade into the background of memory.

In the introduction to this edition I stated that my aim was to show the adoptive process from an **agency perspective**. I hope my remarks will help you see there are others with a vested interest in the successful completion of your child's adoption. **The agency personnel are not your adversaries, they are your allies and friends.** They have a difficult job to do and sometimes things don't always go so well. They are working with many families who all want their children **NOW**. The social worker may feel like a juggler with all the families going round and round through the air. She is trying to keep any and all from falling on the ground. When you call she may seem distracted; in fact, she might not even remember your name.

That doesn't mean she doesn't care; it means only she is busy and she is working under a great deal of stress.

With a little understanding and an appreciation for the complexities of the international adoption process it may be easier for you to remain patient. **Remember, the agency staff is there to help you — they want to see you succeed.**

If you are just beginning this arduous adventure, remember, you do not need to travel it alone. There is a world of support, including agency staff, parent groups, and professionals, who are there to give you assistance. Use them to help you on your way.

I wish you good luck on your search for your child, and share the joy you feel when you will say, **"It was tough, but it was worth it!"**

APPENDICES

---

*The Adoption Letter, a letter explaining who you are and why you want to adopt a child might not be needed in many adoptions. However, some programs and some countries overseas, like to see such a letter from applicants. Therefore we have included a sample letter from a fictious, prospective couple, Roger and Chris Piccolo. Following their adoption is a sample homestudy and psychological report on the same fictious family.

APPENDIX A

ADOPTION TERMINOLOGY

Adopt Abroad — An INS term denoting a requirement for a child to receive an IR-3 visa classification before entering the United States. "Adopt abroad," indicates that both parents (or unmarried parent) have traveled overseas to see the child before bringing the child back to the United States. If the parent is unmarried he/she must be at least 25 years of age. If a married couple, both must be adopting jointly. With an IR-3 visa, the adoption is finalized overseas and it is not necessary (according to INS requirements) for the family to receive post-placements services from their agency (note that although INS might not require such services, they still might be required by the homestudy agency).

Adoption — The process of adding a child to the family through a legal procedure. Once a child is adopted, the parents have complete legal responsibility for the care and welfare of the child. Additional descriptions regarding forms adoption may take, include the following:

Agency Adoption — Utilizing an agency to find the child and bring about the child's adoption.

Direct Adoption (or more commonly, **Parent-Initiated Adoption**) — Refers to an adoption which is initiated by the parents and not the agency. The parents have the overseas contact, prepare their adoption dossier themselves and work directly with an overseas attorney or other child-placing entity. Despite the terminology, an agency is usually involved, if nothing more than for the preparation of the homestudy document. (The word **Direct**, may also indicate a **Private Adoption**).

Domestic Adoption — Refers to adopting a child from within the same country as the family.

143

Foster-Parent Adoption — When a family adopts a child which had previously been placed with them in foster care.

Identified Adoption — Refers to a practice where a family identifies a birthmother for an agency. Once that individual is identified and the agency obtains legal custody of the child it then places for adoption that child with the couple who originally identified the birthmother. In states which prohibit private adoptions (independent adoptions), an identified adoption may be permitted if the birthmother resides in a state other than that of the adoptive parents and obtains the services of a second agency in the state of the birthmother. The second agency must be willing to cooperate with the homestudy agency and to make the placement with the family. In other words, if the second state permits private adoptions and the family complies with correct adoption procedures of the second state, the child can be brought into the parents' state of residency during the postplacement services. The parents would then return to the second state at the conclusion of such services, where the adoption would be finalized.

Linked Adoption — The parents work directly with an overseas entity, but they are referred to this individual or program by an agency. The agency initiates the contact, prepares the documentation and makes the linkage between the family and the child-finding source. Usually the agency is only minimally involved once the parents are working overseas and does not assume responsibility for the success or failure of the overseas portion of the adoption.

Private Adoption — (Independent Adoption, sometimes referred to as Direct Adoption) occurs when the birthparents place their child directly with another family. An attorney, physician or other individual may be used to facilitate or assist the placement and the adoptive family may or may not know the identity of the birthparents. Sometimes adoptive parents search for an infant to adopt by putting an ad in a newspaper or some other tactic. If the result is successful, a private (or independent adoption) ensues. Some states have outlawed the practice of private adoptions, including Michigan, Minnesota, Massachusetts, Delaware, and North Dakota.

Transracial Adoption — Adopting a child who is racially different than the adopting family.

Adopted Child Syndrome—A term with a negative connotation used to describe a cluster of symptoms underlying anti-social behavior such as lying, stealing and other inappropriate behavior.

Adoption Disruption—The dissolution of an adoptive placement. In an adoption disruption the family usually decides the child is "not right for them," and the child is removed from the home. The child will be temporarily placed in foster care until another appropriate adoptive family can be located.

Adoption Exchanges—Organizations which seek to place children who are waiting for adoptive families. They may do this by using a tele-communications network such as the National Adoption Exchange, or by publishing a photolisting book such as The Cap Book. Adoption exchanges can be state or privately run and are organized on a state, regional, national, or specialized basis (see also, photolisting services).

Adoption Facilitator—An individual who assists in facilitating the adoption of a child with a particular family.

Adoption Parent Group (see **Parent Support Group**)

Adoption Search—When an adopted child seeks to locate his or her birthparents. This is a normal desire of many adopted children which usually manifests itself during adolescence.

Black Market Adoption—An illegal adoption. Usually an adoption by-passing the system in which large sums of money are exchanged for a child.

Gray Market Adoption—Refers to a quasi-legal adoption, usually an adoption which bypasses the usual channels and if not completely illegal, comes close to it. The phrase might also be used to describe any adoption which is disapproved of and which somehow does not seem to fit the preconceived idea of what an adoption "ought to be." For example, the speaker might think an adoption from Chile cost too much money. Because of that, when speaking of such an adoption he/she might disparage it by referring to it as a "gray market adoption," when actually, though the adoption was perfectly legal, the speaker didn't believe it should cost so much money and therefore referred to it as "gray market." Actually, an adoption is either legal or illegal.

Homestudy—The written evaluation of an applicant's capacity for parenthood.

> **Homestudy Addendum**—An addition to the original homestudy to reflect a change in circumstance or feelings the family may have with respect to their desire for a type (age, sex, etc.) of child they are willing to accept.

Homestudy Update — Revising a homestudy document so as to make it current and reflect the present day family situation.

Homestudy Agency — The local agency which actually studies the family and prepares the homestudy document.

Intercountry Adoption (International Adoption) — The process of adopting a child from a country other than one's own.

Interstate Compact — The Interstate Compact on the Placement of Children is an agreement by cooperating states which creates an office for monitoring the transferring of children for adoption from one state to another. The Compact was designed so that uniformity of procedures could be established and children as well as parents could be protected from illegal or unethical adoption practices.

INS (Immigration and Naturalization Service) — There are local offices of the INS located throughout the United States. See Appendix E for a list of INS locations.

IR-3 — An INS visa category which indicates that the child has been adopted abroad. Both parents have seen the child overseas and post-placement services will not be required by the Immigration and Naturalization Service.

IR-4 — An INS visa category which indicates that the child's adoption has not been finalized abroad and post-placement services will be required in the United States before a final adoption decree can be rendered.

Legal-Risk Placement — When the child is placed in an adoptive home before the rights of the parents are terminated or during the appeal period after termination of parental rights. The adoptive parents are assuming a "legal-risk" that the birthparents will not change their mind.

Liaison Organization — An organization which is not licensed to prepare homestudy documents or do post-placement supervision, but which can connect a local agency or adopting parents with an overseas child-finding source.

Life Book — A scrapbook with photographs and memorabilia from a child's past. The life-book is a useful device to help an adopted child come to terms with who he/she is and how their past is connected to their present circumstances.

OURS, Inc. (Organization for United Response, 33307 Highway 100 N., Suite 203, Minneapolis, Minnesota 55422) — A parent support group with a national membership and which publishes *OURS Magazine: the Magazine for Adoptive Families.*

Parent Support Group (Adoptive Parent Group) — Parents who have already adopted or are thinking of adopting who get together for mutual support, encouragement and assistance. Many times adoptive parent groups publish newsletters with information and announcements of children who have arrived to join their new families. There are local parent groups and groups which function at a national level, such as OURS, which publishes an extremely informative bi-monthly magazine.

Pre-Adoption Requirements — A stipulation of the Immigration and Naturalization Services which refers to the requirements (state and federal) for adopting a child. To receive an IR-4 visa overseas, INS must receive a statement from the agency that the family has met all of the pre-adoption requirements of their state of residence.

Photo-Listing Service — A book of pictures of waiting children ad sometimes families waiting for children. Photo-listing books are published by State, Private, Regional, National and Specialized Adoption Exchanges which are seeking to find placements for "waiting kids." Examples would include: The Massachusetts Adoption Resource Exchange, which publishes the *MARE Manual* (state exchange), Aid to Adoption of Special Kids (AASK), Rocky Mountain Adoption Exchange (regional), *The Cap Book* (national exchange), National Down's Syndrome Adoption Exchange (specialized).

Post-Placement Services — The services which are provided by the agency after the child is placed with the adoptive family.

Special Needs Child — A child waiting for adoption who has "special" conditions which will require attention. Those conditions can range from relatively minor, easily correctable ones, to serious problems which will demand a great deal of intensified care.

Waiting Child — A child who does not yet have a family and is waiting for a family to adopt him/her.

APPENDIX B

SAMPLE ADOPTION LETTER

To Whom It May Concern:

We are Chris and Roger Piccolo and we very much wish to adopt an infant. Roger is a college graduate and is employed as an insurance adjuster. He is from a family of three children in which he is the middle.

I, (Chris) am a high school graduate who worked as a telephone operator for ten years and have recently been promoted to the position of Service Representitive. I am also a Sunday School teacher where Roger and I attend church and are active members. I am the oldest child in a family of six children.

Roger and I have been married for ten years and have a very happy and stable marriage. We are both Christians and put the Lord first in our lives. We are active in our church. Roger was elected to the Board of Trustees for 1986 and served as Chairman of the Board of Trustees for 1986 and 1987. He is still serving as a board member, but resigned as chairman. I am a member of the Baptist Women, was Children's Coordinator for 1985 and 1986 and am currently a member of the Nursery Committee.

Since we were first married, we have been trying to have children, though unsuccessfully. Roger has been diagnosed as having a low sperm count and I have had to undergo surgery. For the last two years we have been taking a drug called Clomid. I think we have finally come to accept that it is not in the Lord's will for us to biologically have children. Therefore we would like very much to adopt, since we believe we both have a great capacity for love and room in our home to share with a little one.

We live in a nice neighborhood, only one mile from an elementary school. We have a large backyard and much room for a child to play. We are buying our home and it is large enough that a child would have his or her own room.

My interests are sewing, gardening, yard work and canning fruits and vegetables. We both enjoy camping, canoeing, and attending church and community events.

We have a loving and good marriage and would do everything we could to give our child the happiest life possible. We appreciate your help in making our dream come true. I am enclosing a photograph of ourselves and our home.

Anything you could do on our behalf is gratefully appreciated.

Sincerely,

Chris and Roger Piccolo

APPENDIX C

ADOPTIVE HOMESTUDY
(Children's Hope Adoption Services)

CASE NAME: Piccolo, Chris and Roger
ADDRESS: 7982 S. Whitney Road
COUNTY: Shepherd, MI 48883
TELEPHONE: (517) 828-9381
WORKER: Barbara T. Burns
APPROVAL DATE: 01/12/88

Dates of Contact:

11/11/87: Telephone contact to set up interview time.
11/26/87: Orientation/Assessment Interview
12/02/87: Homestudy Interview and Home Visit, Mr. and Mrs. Piccolo
12/16/87: Homestudy Interview, Mrs. Piccolo
12/23/87: Homestudy Interview, Mr. Piccolo
01/10/87: Homestudy Interview, Mr. and Mrs. Piccolo

Child Desired

Chris and Roger Piccolo are requesting to adopt an infant, 0-12 months of age. Either male or female would be acceptable for this family. They prefer a basically healthy child but could adopt a child with a low birth weight or low apgar score. A child with a minor correctable handicap would also be appropriate for this family.

The Piccolo's wish to adopt a child of Oriental/Hispanic, Oriental/Black, Hispanic, Hispanic/Indian, Indian, or Anglo ethnicity.

Both Chris and Roger plan to travel to their child's country to learn about the culture and to bring their child home.

151

Parents

Born **Roger R. Piccolo** on 1/19/56 (verified #223) in Kalamazoo, Michigan. Roger is the middle child of three. He has one older brother and one younger brother. He is very close to both. He has happy childhood memories and describes his younger years as structured and active.

Roger is employed with General Adjustment Bureau as an insurance adjuster. His service area is throughout northeast Michigan in a three county area. Although the company office is in Alpena, Roger provides services for Clare, Gladwin and Ogemaw Counties. Roger reports that even though he obtains a lot of satisfaction from his current occupation, he eventually would like to return to school and achieve his teaching certification. He plans to attend Central Michigan University on a part-time basis in the near future.

Roger's father started as a plumber/pipefitter. In his mid 40's, his father changed careers to own his own sales representative company. Roger recalls him as assertive with a clear sense of values. He was a go-getter who frequently worked long hours. Roger describes his mother as the motivating force in his life. She was a hard working woman who worked at home. Discipline, usually administered by his father, was verbal reprimands. Roger states that his parents had a good marriage, were good friends to each other.

Roger's father died in 1970 and his mother remains single. He keeps in frequent contact and helps her out with maintenance and business decisions.

Roger feels a peace with himself and says that all that is lacking in his family life is a child.

Christine Lee (Suggs) Piccolo, born in St. Paul, Minnesota on 9/23/57 (verified # 122-87-1595). She is the oldest child in a family of six children. She has one younger sister and four younger brothers. She recalls her growing years as filled with love, God and family closeness.

Christine has been employed with the General Telephone Company for the past ten years. She has just recently advanced from a switchboard operator position to a service representative. Prior to the Piccolo's move to Shepherd, Chris worked out of the G.T.E. office in Harrison. Now she works from the office in Alma.

Chris's father was an elementary school teacher. Her mother worked at home. Chris states that her parents' marriage is very solid. She remembers her parents as church and family oriented. They spent all non-working hours together and Chris does not remember them being ever apart. One of Chris's favorite family activities were the family vacation trips. Both parents shared the responsibility of discipline. Chris can never remember being spanked.

Chris still keeps close ties with her family. She and Roger live only ten minutes from her parents and she sees her parents frequently. They all attend the same church and Chris co-teaches Sunday School class with her mother.

Chris is very content with herself, her career and her marriage. She is optimistic about what the future holds for her.

Marital Relationship

Roger and Chris have been married since June of 1978. They met when Roger, as a college student, rented an upstairs apartment in the home of Chris's parents. After dating for about one year Roger and Chris became engaged and married six months later. Both Chris and Roger share equally in their responsibilities for their home which includes both cooking and cleaning. The Piccolo's characterize their marriage as being very warm, caring and communicative. They feel that their different styles of functioning complement each other and report similar values and ways of thinking. Roger and Chris feel that they would like to extend their love and caring to a child and in time would like to complete their family with yet another child. Both Piccolos expressed their enjoyment of children and felt that two children would complete their family.

Life Style

Chris and Roger Piccolo are very involved in their church and community activities. They are members of the First Baptist Church and attend faithfully. Both are members of weekly men's/women's groups at their church. They serve as leaders for the teen group and Chris co-teaches Sunday School with her mother for sixth graders.

The Piccolos are very service oriented and strongly believe in doing their part to make the world a better place. They sponsor a foster child in Central America and participate in a community service project designed to teach adults to read.

The Piccolo's leisure time is usually spent in giving their time and talent to their church and community. They also enjoy walks, travel and dinner with friends.

Occupation, Educational Level and Aspirations

Chris is a high school graduate, having attended the Gregory Cortez High School in Alpena. She is gainfully employed as service representative with the General Telephone Company. Although her job and house give her a great deal of satisfaction, she plans to return to school and obtain a college degree.

Roger has been an insurance adjuster with the General Adjustment Bureau for the past ten years. He states that he likes his work and takes it seriously. If the opportunity presents itself, he would like to return to Central Michigan University and obtain certification for teaching. Roger says he would like to be an elementary school teacher.

Personality and Physical Description

Roger is 5'11" tall and weighs 160 lbs. and is in good physical condition. He has dark brown curly hair. He has an outgoing and sincere manner. Throughout our interviews, he was cooperative, honest and sincere.

Chris has a cheerful and optimistic nature. In conversation, she is friendly, warm and has a good sense of humor. She is 5'8" tall and at 125 lbs. has a slender build. Chris has brown hair, hazel eyes and has worn glasses since she was eight years old.

Health of Adoptive Parents

According to medical forms, Roger and Chris Piccolo are in good physical condition. There is no known medical reason why the Piccolos should not be considered for an adoptive placement.

Both Roger and Chris have been diagnosed as being infertile. The Piccolos have undergone corrective surgery as well as treatment with the drug Clomid. At the present time, Roger remains with a low sperm count and it is uncertain as to whether or not Chris's surgery has been successful.

Psychological evaluations prove Roger and Chris to be emotionally healthy and ready to undertake the role of parenthood. They are of an age to be compatible with the raising of a young child. Neither have been treated for mental illness or emotional problems.

Economic Situation

The Piccolo's have a gross annual income of $35,000. Net monthly expenses are:

House:	$784	Insurance:	
Utilities:	80	Car:	$900
Phone:	20	House:	450
Groceries:	200		

The Piccolo's are buying their home and currently have a mortgage of $60,000. Current market value for their home is estimated at $115,000. They have a savings account of $7,000.

Roger has life insurance coverage in the amount of $90,000. Their health insurance is through Pension Group Services and includes any children they might adopt.

The Piccolo's appear to be financially sound and manage their money responsibly. They earn sufficient income to financially provide for a child.

Housing

Roger and Chris live in a two story blue colored duplex. They live on a suburban street filled with neat, well maintained homes. Their home includes a small kitchen, 1½ bathrooms and a combination dining/living room. Upstairs there are 3 roomy bedrooms and plenty of storage area. The basement is unfinished and is ideal for roller skating and bike riding on rainy days.

There is also a two stall attached garage. Outdoors, there is 13,000 square feet of an unfenced, neat trimmed yard. Their neighborhood consists of many families with young children and there are several parks not far away. Roger and Chris rent out the other side of their duplex. Their current tenants have a five year old daughter. Housekeeping standards are excellent. The Piccolo's home has a comfortable atmosphere and is immaculate. They have one pet, a Collie dog named Gus.

Parenting Skills

Roger and Chris Piccolo feel that they are at a point in their lives where children would add to their lives. Since their discovery of their infertility three years ago, they have considered adoption.

They have undergone much planning and preparation in regards to this adoption. They have saved money, read books, and discussed the pros and cons of adoption with adoptive parents. It is their strong belief that an adopted, foreign born child, will find total acceptance and love from themselves, their extended family and their racially mixed community. All friends and relatives have lent their complete support for this adoption.

The Piccolos believe that structure and supervision are important aspects of child rearing. They plan to be involved in their child's life and establish an open but firm relationship with him/her.

Roger and Chris also expressed the need of a child to be loved and supported throughout their lives. They plan to use verbal reprimands and privilege-taking as methods of discipline. They state that physical punishment should be used only as a last resort.

The Piccolos state that a child will help complete their marriage. They plan to raise their child with the full knowledge of his/her adoption. They will answer all questions to the best of their ability. If asked, they plan to tell the child that his/her parents were unable to care for any child at that time. Out of their love for him/her, they gave him/her to a loving couple who vigorously sought after him/her.

They do not feel threatened by the biological parents and empathize with their painful decision.

The Piccolos understand and accept the risks involved in an international adoption. They do not anticipate their child will physically resemble them and they don't have any rigid expectations for him/her. They plan to study their child's cultural heritage and incorporate some of that knowledge into their family's own lifestyle and tradition. They realize that they may have little or no medical information on the child or his/her birth parents and have considered the fact that their child may have health problems at the time of placement. They are also aware of the possibility of their child developing a previously undiagnosed health problem. They are accepting of this and willing to take that risk. The Piccolos will assume full financial and medical responsibility for their child's needs after placement. They are willing to know and understand the laws of Michigan pertaining to international adoption, the stipulations of the Immigration and Naturalization Service, the delays caused by Interstate Compact procedures and the adoption process in general.

Readiness to Adopt

Following the Piccolo's initial assessment/orientation interviewed, they signed the "Statement of Understand," indicating that the policies of Children's Hope had been explained to them and that they were aware of the risks involved in pursuing an international adoption. After making a decision to continue, they proceeded to their homestudy interviews with their social service worker. During that time, they followed a systematic approach to international adoptions and became informed on cross cultural parenting by studying texts and following the checklist provided by Children's Hope.

Once the child is placed in their home, Chris plans to take a leave of absence or quit her job all together to ease the transition into their new life. Roger also intends to take time off so he will have more time for his family.

Police Clearance

Roger and Chris Piccolo indicated they have never been arrested on their application form. Michigan State Police clearance forms confirm this to be a true statement.

References

Person's Contacted:

Rev. and Mrs. Larry Hart, 2419 Maple Way, Kalamazo, MI 49009
Robert Sicignano, Leisure Time Village, Sarasota, FL 33581
Dr. and Mrs. Russ Womsey, 925 Dalton Road, Alpena, MI 49025

All references showered praise and affection for the Piccolos and their efforts to adopt. They were described as: "committed, consistent and stable." Everyone agreed they would be excellent candidates for an adoptive placement.

Social Worker's Impressions and Recommendations

It appears to this worker, that Roger and Chris Piccolo have a solid and loving marriage. They are in good physical condition. Both Roger and Chris's employment appears secure and they are financially stable.

Children's Hope, and this worker, recommends placement with Roger and Chris Piccolo, a child between the ages of 0-12 months. Either sex would be appropriate. Their child should be basically healthy, although a minor correctable handicap was well as some mild behavioral or emotional problems would be acceptable for this family.

Barbara T. Burns	Martha S. Green
Social Service Worker	Social Service Supervisor

APPENDIX D

PSYCHOLOGICAL EVALUATION

Robert M. Bunting, M.A.
Temporary Limited Licensed Psychologist
952 South University
Mt. Pleasant, MI 48858

MR. ROGER PICCOLO was seen on 1/5/87. At that time a psychological interview and Incomplete Sentence Test were administered.

Mr. Piccolo is a thirty-one year old male Caucasian who is six foot, eleven inches tall and weights approximately 160 pounds. He appeared at the interview in casual clothes, i.e., slacks and a sports shirt and was neatly groomed.

Throughout the interviewing process, Mr. Piccolo appeared at ease and was very forthcoming with his responses. He attended to the questions which were asked and elaborated upon each one without hesitation.

Mr. Piccolo appears to be a very outgoing, warm young man. His sense of responsibility as well as his gregariousness suggests a more mature level of functioning than his chronological age indicates. He seems attuned to both his own and other peoples' feelings and is sensitive to them. Mr. Piccolo's greatest strength lies within his ability to communicate with people which he does with ease. He possesses a characteristic which is often missing in "traditional" males, that being a nurturing quality, which seems to underlie much of his functioning. This was noted as he addressed his relationship with his wife. This characteristic seems attributable to his relationship to his mother, to whom he feels he is closest.

Mr. Piccolo's long range goals and optimism for the future suggest that he is continuing to grow both occupationally and interpersonally.

159

Although Mr. Piccolo's present job seems to be fairly secure and stable, he stressed a need to advance himself so that he could provide even more for his family and for the people he worked with. As a result, Mr. Piccolo has made plans to pursue a Master's degree in Early Elementary Education from Central Michigan University. This clearly reflects a commitment to change and grow.

Overall, Mr. Piccolo seems to be an easygoing, sociable young man, who enjoys being with people. He presets as a loving husband who speaks openly of his love and adoration of his wife and his commitment to their relationship. His major anxieties seem to revolve around his work performance, although, according to Mr. Piccolo, he is often praised by his supervisors for his work.

Mrs. Christine Lee Piccolo was interviewed on 1/9/87.

Mrs. Piccolo is a thirty-year-old female Caucasian, who is five feet, eight inches tall and weighs approximately 125 pounds. She appeared at the interview neatly dressed and groomed, which included facial makeup.

Mrs. Piccolo was clearly anxious throughout much of the interview. She was hesitant to complete the required tasks and initially responded in a very guarded manner. In an effort to break through her resistance, Mrs. Piccolo was directly confronted, which involved describing her behavior to her. After a few minutes Mrs. Piccolo discussed various things she had been told regarding adoption studies, stating she was afraid she might "say the wrong thing." Although this may have added to Mrs. Piccolo's tentativeness, this characteristic seems to underlie much of her social functioning, particularly when she is anxious. Her past relationship with her father, which seemed to be of a cold, distant nature has taken it's toll on Mrs. Piccolo. As a child she was frequently told by her father that she was not good enough or pretty enough, which has left her with a low self-esteem further adding to her "shyness." Although Mrs. Piccolo presents as a shy somewhat withdrawn woman, her overall functioning has not curtailed her work performance as she has currently moved from a Operator's position with the phone company to a Service Representative. This, as well as her response to my comments early in the interview reflects a capacity for change when environmental demands are placed upon her.

Mrs. Piccolo's relationship with her husband has seemed to provide her with a warm loving environment which she lacked with her father. Roger has helped to enhance her personal growth. She seems aware of her personal difficulties, and although she has attempted to work through her problems with her husband, Mrs. Piccolo indicated an interest in seeking professional assistance.

Although Mrs. Piccolo finds it difficult to discuss herself she openly talked about her relationship with Mr. Piccolo. It was apparent from her discussion that she is capable of a warm, loving relationship which she has given not only to her husband but to the children of her sister and brothers as well. Mrs. Piccolo has to a degree been able to give to other's what she was unable to receive from her paternal relationship, which seems attributable to the nurturing relationship she has with her husband. She remains close with her mother and share a teaching role with her mother at her local church. Mrs. Piccolo also seems committed to her role as a wife, prospective mother and active participant in her church activities. Mrs. Piccolo's strengths lie in her sense of caring and concern for others as well as her continued striving for further personal growth.

The Piccolo's seem to be very secure in their relationship. They exhibited a sense of caring and concern for one another as well as a deep regard and respect for each individual's functioning. Their relationship seems to provide for each of the Piccolos the very thing they missed during their childhood ie; Roger a sense of family and Chris a nurturing male relationship. Both are supportive of each other's personal and occupational growth and actively work to enhance their overall functioning. Mr. and Mrs. Piccolo have each addressed their own and each other's inability to conceive and seem able to deal with this issue.

Each of Piccolo's in their own way, displayed a degree of love and caring which could readily be extended to a child. Together they seem able to provide a stable, nurturing environment for a child or an infant. The placement of an infant or a child within this home would provide much for both the child and the Piccolos. Both Piccolos have exhibited their desire to have a child through laborious and extensive medical procedures which were unsuccessful. Each seem prepared to make the various sacrifices which are inherent when one raises a child and seem to be looking forward to the challenges in rearing a child. The Piccolos, as a couple, have continued to grow and seem able to extend their love and caring to a child.

It is felt that the Piccolos would make fine parents and that a child or infant in their family will be beneficial for all. Therefore, I am recommending both Christine and Roger Piccolo as adoptive parents.

Robert M. Bunting, M.A.
Temporary Limited Licensed
Psychologist

Maralyn Janes
Licensed Psychologist

APPENDIX E

IMMIGRATION AND NATURALIZATION SERVICES OFFICES*

District Offices in the United States

Anchorage, AK 99513
New Federal Bldg.
701 C Street, RM D-251
Lock Box 16

Atlanta, GA 30303
Richard B. Russell
Federal Office Bldg.
75 Spring Street, S.W.
Room 1408

Baltimore, MD 21201
E.A. Garmatz Federal Bldg.
101 West Lombard Street

Boston, MA 02203
John Fitzgerald Kennedy
Federal Bldg.
Government Center

Buffalo, NY 14202
68 Court Street

Chicago, IL 60604
Dirksen Federal Office Bldg.
219 South Dearborn Street

Cleveland, OH 44199
RM 1917
Anthony J. Celebreeze
Federal Office Bldg.
1240 East 9th Street

Dallas, TX 75242
RM 6A21, Federal Bldg.
1100 Commerce Street

Denver, CO 80202
1787 Federal Bldg.
1961 Stout Street

Detroit, MI 48207
Federal Bldg.
333 Mt. Elliott Street

El Paso, TX 79984
343 U.S. Courthouse
P.O. Box 9398

Harlingen, TX 78550
2102 Teege Road

Hartford, CT 06103-3060
Ribicoff Federal Bldg.
450 Main Street

---

*The Immigration of Adopted and Prospective Adoptive Children, Dept. of Justice, Immigration and Naturalization Service form M-249 (Washington, D.C.: Government Printing Office, 1984), pp. 23-25.

Helena, MT 59626
Federal Bldg., RM 512
310 South Park, Drawer 10036

Honolulu, HI 96809
P.O. Box 461
595 Ala Moana Blvd.

Houston, TX 77004
2627 Caroline Street

Kansas City, MO 64106
Suite 1100
324 East Eleventh Street

Los Angeles, CA 90012
300 North Los Angeles Street

Miami, FL 33138
7880 Biscayne Blvd.

Newark, NJ 07102
Federal Bldg.
970 Broad Street

New Orleans, LA 70113
Postal Service Bldg.
RM T-8005
701 Loyola Avenue

New York, NY 10278
26 Federal Plaza

Omaha, NE 68102
Federal Office Bldg.
RM 1008
106 South 15th Street

Philadelphia, PA 19106
U.S. Courthouse, RM 1321
Independence Mall West
601 Market Street

Phoenix, AZ 85025
Federal Bldg.
230 North First Avenue

Portland, ME 04112
76 Pearl Street

Portland, OR 97209
Federal Office Bldg.
511 N.W. Broadway

St. Paul, MN 55101
927 Main Post Office Bldg.
180 East Kellogg Blvd.

San Antonio, TX 78206
U.S. Federal Bldg.
Suite A301
727 East Durango

San Diego, CA 92188
880 Front Street

San Francisco, CA 94111
Appraisers Bldg.
630 Sansome Street

San Juan, PR 00936
GPO Box 5068

Seattle, WA 98134
815 Airport Way, South

Washington, DC 20013
25 E Street, N.W.
P.O. Box 37034

Other Service Offices in the United States

Agana, GU 96910
801 Pacific News Bldg.
238 O'Hara Street

Albany, NY 12207
RM 220
U.S. Post Office & Courthouse
445 Broadway

Albuquerque, NM 87103
Federal Bldg., U.S. Courthouse
RM 5512, 500 Gold Avenue, S.W.
Box 567

Charleston, SC 29403
Federal Bldg., RM 330
334 Meeting Street

Charlotte, NC 28205
1111 Hawthorne Lane

Charlotte Amalie
St. Thomas, VI 00801
Federal Bldg.
P.O. Box 610

Christiansted, St. Croix,
VI 00850
P.O. Box 1270 Kingshill

Cincinnati, OH 45201
U.S. Post Office &
 Courthouse
100 East 5th Street
P.O. Box 537

Fresno, CA 93721
U.S. Courthouse
Federal Bldg., RM 1308
1130 O Street

Indianapolis, IN 46204
RM 148
46 East Ohio Street

Jacksonville, FL 32201
311 West Monroe Street
RM 227, Post Office Bldg.
P.O. Box 4608

Las Vegas, NV 89101
Federal Bldg., U.S. Courthouse
300 Las Vegas Blvd. South

Louisville, KY 40202
RM 601, U.S. Courthouse Bldg.
West 6th & Broadway

Memphis, TN 38103
814 Federal Office Bldg.
167 North Main Street

Merrillville, IN 46410
51 West 80th Place
Georgetown Plaza

Milwaukee, WI 53202
RM 186, Federal Bldg.
517 East Wisconsin Avenue

Norfolk, VA 23510
Norfolk Federal Bldg.
RM 439, 200 Granby Mall

Oklahoma City, OK 73102
RM 4423, 200 N.W. 4th St.
Federal Bldg. & Courthouse

Pittsburgh, PA 15222
2130 Federal Bldg.
1000 Liberty Avenue

Providence, RI 02903
Federal Bldg.
U.S. Post Office
Exchange Terrace

Reno, NV 89502
Suite 150
350 South Center Street

St. Albans, VT 05478
Federal Bldg.
P.O. Box 328

St. Louis, MO 63101
RM 100
210 North Tucker Blvd.

Salt Lake City, UT 84101
230 West 400 South Street

San Jose, CA 95113
280 South First Street

Spokane, WA 99201
691 U.S. Courthouse Bldg.

Tampa, FL 33602
RM 539
500 Zack Street

Tuscon, AZ 85701
RM 8-M, Federal Bldg.
301 W. Congress

REFERENCES

Chapter Two

Cameron, Nancy. "A View From the Other Side." *OURS: The Magazine of Adoptive Families,* November/December 1986, p. 6.

Erichsen, Heino. "International Adoption and the Media." *Los Ninos News,* March 1987, pp. 1-3.

National Committee for Adoption. *Adoption Factbook: United States Data, Issues, Regulations and Resources.* Washington, D.C.: National Committee for Adoption, 1985.

Pahz, James. "Building Families Through International Adoption." *International Quarterly of Community Health Education,* 8, No. 1 (1987-1988), pp. 91-97.

Pilotti, Francisco J. "Intercountry Adoption: A View From Latin America." *Child Welfare: Journal of the Child Welfare League of America,* LXIV, No. 1 (1985), pp. 25-35.

Chapter Three

Erichsen, Heino. "International Adoption and the Media." *Los Ninos News,* March 1987, pp. 1-3.

Chapter Four

Darby, Richard. *Direct or Parent-Initiated Intercountry Adoptions.* Rev. Phyllis Loewenstein. Newton, Mass: International Adoptions, 1978.

Green, Lawrence W., and C.L. Anderson. *Community Health.* 5th ed. St. Louis: Times Mirror/Mosby, 1986.

Rosenbaum, Betsey R. *Intercountry Adoption Guidelines.* The American Public Welfare Association. Washington, D.C.: U.S. Government Printing Office, 1980.

Chapter Five

Kim, David H. *Prayer for Latin America.* Eugene, OR: Holt International Children's Services, 1987.

Report on Foreign Adoption. Boulder, CO: International Concerns Committee for Children, 1987.

Chapter Six

Cameron, Nancy. "A View From the Other Side." *OURS: The Magazine of Adoptive Families,* November/December 1986, p. 6.

Lange, Robert W., MD, MPH, and Ellen Warnock-Eckhart, MSW. "Selected Infectious Disease Risks in International Adoptees." *The Pediatric Infectious Disease Journal*, 6, No. 3 (1987), pp. 447-450.

Los Ninos International Handbook. Austin, Texas: Los Ninos International Adoption Center, 1986.

Pahz, James, and Cheryl Pahz. *Children's Hope Handbook: Policies and Procedures.* 4th ed. Shepherd, MI: Children's Hope Adoption Services, 1987.

Report on Foreign Adoption. Boulder, CO: International Concerns Committee for Children, 1987.

Chapter Seven

Immigration of Adopted and Prospective Adoptive Children. Dept. of Justice, Immigration and Naturalization Service Form M-249. Washington, D.C.: Government Printing Office, 1984.

Pahz, James, and Cheryl Pahz. *Children's Hope Handbook: Policies and Procedures.* 4th ed. Shepherd, MI: Children's Hope Adoption Services, 1987.

Chapter Eight

Pahz, James, and Cheryl Pahz. *Children's Hope Handbook: Policies and Procedures.* 4th ed. Shepherd, MI: Children's Hope Adoption Services, 1987.

Chapter Nine

Pahz, James, and Cheryl Pahz. *Children's Hope Handbook: Policies and Procedures.* 4th ed. Shepherd, MI: Children's Hope Adoption Services, 1987.

Chapter Ten

Perez, Herman, and Sam Modello. "Customs of Courtesy Most Commonly Used In Colombia." Handout originally provided Peace Corps Workers in 1977.

Chapter Eleven

Gabriel, Susan. "Michigan Committee Wins Discrimination Case." *The Children's Voice,* March 1986, pp. 1-2.

Grabe, Pamela V., ed. *Adoption Resources For Mental Health Professionals.* Mercer, PA: The Children's Aid Society in Mercer County, 1986.

Harris-Warren, Mary Ellen. "A Case Study of Foreign Street Children's Adjustment and Assimilation into American Culture." Diss. Univ. of Connecticut, 1984.

Klagsbrun, Francine. "Debunking the 'Adopted Child Syndrome' Myth." *OURS: The Magazine of Adoptive Families,* July/August 1987, pp. 20-21.

Silverman, Arnold Richard. "Transracial Adoption in the United States: A Study of Assimilation and Adjustment." Diss. Univ. of Wisconsin, 1986.

Williams, John E., and J. Kenneth Morland. *Race, Color, and the Young Child.* Chapel Hill: Univ. of North Carolina Press, 1976.

Chapter Twelve

Boyd, William C.C., M.D., and Huntington Sheldon, M.D., *An Introduction to the Study of Disease.* 6th ed. Philadelphia: Lea and Febiger, 1977.

Green, Lawrence W., and C.L. Anderson. *Community Health.* 5th ed. St. Louis: Times Mirror/Mosby, 1986.

Hershow, Ronald C., MD, Stephen C. Hadler, MD, and Mark A. Kane, MD. "Adoption of Children From Countries with Endemic Hepatitis B: Transmission Risk and Medical Issues." *The Pediatric Infectious Diseases Journal,* 6, No. 5 (1987), pp. 431-437.

Jenista, Jerri Ann, M.D. "AIDS: A Growing Spectre." A Paper Presented at Project Orphans Abroad: Opportunities in Adoption. Cleveland, Ohio, September 11-12, 1987.

Jenista, Jerri Ann, M.D. "AIDS and Internationally Adopted Children." *OURS: The Magazine of Adoptive Families,* July/August 1987, pp. 14-15.

Jenista, Jerri Ann, M.D., and Daniel Chapman, M.D. "Medical Problems of Foreign-Born Adopted Children." *American Journal of Diseases of Children,* 141 (1987), 298-302.

Lange, W. Robert, MD, MPH, and Ellen Warnock-Eckhart, MSW. "Selected Infectious Disease Risks in International Adoptees." *The Pediatric Infectious Disease Journal,* 6, No. 5 (1987), 447-450.

Mann, Jonathan M. "The Global AIDS Situation." *World Health: The Magazine of the World Health Organization,* June 1987, pp. 6-8.

Seligmann, Jean, with Gary Esolen, Richard Sandza and Deborah Witherspoon. "The Unmentionable Disease." *Newsweek,* 31 January 1983, p. 67.

Wallis, Claudia. (As reported by Patricia Delaney, Joyce Leviton, and Mellissa Ludtke). "AIDS: A Growing Threat." *Time,* 12 August 1986, pp. 40-47.

Welsbacher, Anne. "Assessing Your Child's Health Needs." *OURS: The Magazine of Adoptive Families,* July/August 1987, pp. 12-13.

Zelnick, Charles J., MD. "Hepatitis B and Overseas Adoption." *Adoption Today,* 6, No. 1 (1986), pp. 25-27.

INDEX